B. M. Lawrence

Celestial Sonnets

A collection of new and original songs and hymns of peace and progress

B. M. Lawrence

Celestial Sonnets

A collection of new and original songs and hymns of peace and progress

ISBN/EAN: 9783337083519

Printed in Europe, USA, Canada, Australia, Japan

Cover: Foto ©Thomas Meinert / pixelio.de

More available books at **www.hansebooks.com**

CELESTIAL SONNETS.

A COLLECTION OF

New and Original Songs and Hymns of

Peace and Progress.

DESIGNED FOR

PUBLIC GATHERINGS, HOME CIRCLES,

RELIGIOUS, SPIRITUAL, TEMPERANCE,

SOCIAL AND CAMP MEETINGS, ETC.

BY

B. M. LAWRENCE, M.D.

Copyright, 1886, by B. M. LAWRENCE, M.D.

PREFACE.

In preparing CELESTIAL SONNETS, the desire of the author has been to meet the growing demand for an entirely new and original book of Spiritual, Temperance, and Progressive Songs, with simple, appropriate music easily arranged, having suitable choruses for home, circles, social or public gatherings. While the aim has been to avoid everything of a purely sectarian character, it will be seen that only the highest moral principles have been inculcated, and it is believed that by adopting this plan, the wonderful power of music will become a still greater blessing to mankind; and that the book will more effectively console the sorrowing with the hope of happy reunions; comfort the care-worn toiler with greater assurance of a final full reward; refine and purify the affections; rekindle latent loves of home and country; harmonize conflicting creeds and opinions; counteract the cold chilling waves of materialism; unfold the higher moral and spiritual faculties; assist in developing a scientific religion of evolution, and help eventually to discover the "missing links" in the great chain of human sympathies which will at last unite all nations and people in one grand effort to secure "Peace on earth and good will to men." One feature of the words is the effort made to frequently enforce the teaching of that greatly neglected text: "Whatsoever a man soweth that shall he also reap;" a grand truth that cannot be too often repeated, either in song or story. This sentiment of absolute justice we have interblended with that most beautiful belief that the soul still lives when the body dies, and that "loved ones gone before us" can, and do return; that they become our guardian angels, inciting us to lead true and noble lives; that by our good works here, we can lay up treasures "over there," and have more beautiful "mansions" prepared for us in "The sweet land of sunshine." When these celestial soul-cheering truths are sung, taught and practiced daily in every home, they will take away the sting of death and banish all fear of the grave; love and peace will reign supreme; heaven will begin on earth, and "The world will be the better for it."

The book contains one hundred and twenty-eight pages, nearly the same number of songs, with about seventy-five entirely new pieces of music, a great many choruses and a few old standard selections. Some of the words are adapted to popular airs, and the tunes to the songs marked G. H., can be found in GOSPEL HYMNS.

We are under great obligations to friends for kindly aiding us, and to those who have contributed to the work, for their valuable compositions. While actively engaged in professional duties, we have taken time and been to great expense in writing and publishing the Sonnets, and would call attention to the fact that we have secured the copyright for both the words and music of almost every piece, and to reprint either, without permission, would be an infringement of the copyright, and treated accordingly.

We desire to express our special thanks to Mess. J. M. ARMSTRONG & Co., for the care and general interest taken in the Music Typography, also to Mr. George Beaverson for much valuable assistance in arranging the music.

DEDICATION. To all who love the truth and desire to promote harmony, health, happiness and peace; the CELESTIAL SONNETS are most cordially inscribed by

THE AUTHOR.

CELESTIAL SONNETS.

Sweet Summer Home.

"In my father's house are many mansions."—John 14:2.

B. M. L. B. M. LAWRENCE.

1. Sweet home a-bove, sweet home of love, Thou fair land of the free,
2. Sweet home a-bove, sweet home of love, Where no more storms a-rise,
3. Sweet home a-bove, sweet home of love, Be-yond the si-lent tomb,

Cho. Sweet home a-bove, sweet home of love, No more shall grief or gloom

We love to feel that ev'-ry soul May find sweet rest in thee;
Nor tear-drops fall, nor dark-ness pall The ev-er smil-ing skies,
How sweet to know, while here be-low, In heav'n we have a home.

Nor want nor care dis-turb us there, Where all is peace at home.

We've no a-bid-ing cit-y here, But seek for one to come,
By faith, the pure in heart be-hold That land where an-gels roam,
The joys of life are oft-en bright, Yet chill-ing blasts will come;

And tho' our way be dark and drear There's light and peace at home.
Where hopes ne'er die, nor loves grow cold, In that e-ter-nal home.
But, oh! we long to see the light Of that sweet sum-mer home.

Inside the Golden Gate.

R. M. LAWRENCE, M.D.   Miss M. W. M.

3.

Source of Love, in faith we plead,
Grant us this—Thou knowest we need
Trust in Thee, a constant friend,
One on whom we may depend.
In each dark and trying hour,
Make us feel the soothing power
Of dear friends who for us wait,
Safe inside the Golden Gate.

4.

Source of Wisdom, Love and Truth,
Fountain of immortal youth,
Living waters for the mind,
Grant that we may seek and find.
When we help the downcast rise,
We build mansions in the skies,
Where sweet angels for us wait,
Safe inside the Golden Gate.

The Pilgrim's Invocation.

B. M. LAWRENCE, M. D. Miss M. W. M.

2.
Make me feel my heart lies open
  To the gaze of loved ones gone;
That before the lips have spoken,
  Unto them my thoughts are known.
Every day while drawing nearer
  To that land of endless youth,
May Thy voice to me speak clearer,
  Words of wisdom, love and truth.

3.
Search my heart, its weakness show me,
  Draw it still to Thee more near;
Teach me while on earth to know Thee,
  And to find sweet Heaven here.
Grant to guide me, great Jehovah,
  Lead me with light from above;
Guide the Pilgrim passing over
  To the peaceful land of love.

Angels there will welcome thee.

B. M. LAWRENCE, M. D. Miss M. W. M.

3
"Check those founts of anguish streaming,
Most of life's ills are but seeming,
Darkest clouds have silver gleaming
If thine eyes could only see,
Far beyond the mystic river,
Where the soul is young forever,
We shall meet to part,—no, never—
Angels bring these thoughts to thee.

4
" Banish all thy grief and sorrow,
Fear not,—trust the coming morrow,
Working, wait and hope on, for oh,
Think what shall the harvest be.
In that land of endless morning,
When the soul shall cease its longing,
Golden days for thee are dawning,
Angels there will welcome thee."

That Glorious Rest.

B. M. L.　　　　　　　　　　　　　　　　　　B. M. LAWRENCE, M.D.

There is a rest a-wait-ing for me, And my hopes are cen-tered there;
The great may boast of their worldly gains, And the rich in splen-dors roll,

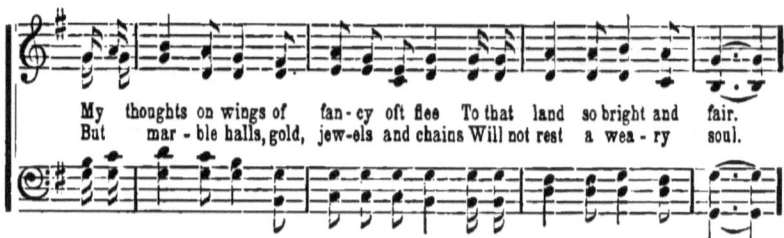

My thoughts on wings of fan-cy oft flee To that land so bright and fair.
But mar-ble halls, gold, jew-els and chains Will not rest a wea-ry soul.

Chorus.

That rest, that rest, that glo-ri-ous rest, So sweet does it seem in my dreams;

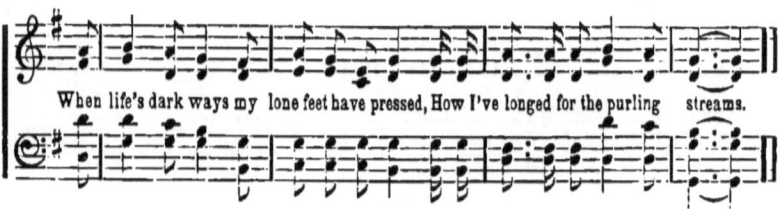

When life's dark ways my lone feet have pressed, How I've longed for the purling streams.

3
Sweet bards may sing of a sunny clime,
Where the skies are clear and bright,
But there are scenes more grandly sublime
In that land of love and light.

4
Bright land of beauty and sunshine so fair,
Where our friends are with the blest,
And they wait to welcome us over there,
In that world of peace and rest.

Sweet Home by the River.

B. M. L.
B. M. LAWRENCE, M. D.

1. In the soul-world are mansions Of peace and delight;
   There, dear ones are waiting All robed in pure white,
   And they sing sweetest anthems Of love on that shore,
   In their home by the river, Where night is no more.

2. Crystal hills 'round the mansions So gracefully rise,
   Like azure-clad mountains, They blend with the skies;
   There the rainbows of promise Remain all the year,
   Near that home by the river, Sweet soul rest so dear.

3. All the fields 'round those mansions Are waving with gold,
   There life-plants with love-bloom In beauty unfold;
   And there fruits grow immortal On evergreen trees,
   Sweet, sweet home by the river, We love thee for these.

4
All our friends in those mansions
Are faithful and true,
We love them more dearly
Than blossoms love dew;
Like the field-blooming lilies,
And as free from all care,
In that home by the river
Are the dear loved ones there.

5
For a place in those mansions,
With title made clear,
A mountain of diamonds
Were treasures less dear;
There life is all pleasure,
And the weary find rest
In that home by the river,—
Fair land of the blest.

Angels Sing Once Again.

B. M. LAWRENCE, M. D.   M. W. M.

1. Those we love who have passed through the vale
Can re-turn; life at death does not cease; This grand
truth let the peo-ple all hail, With a
shout as the hand-maid of peace.

2. They or-dain that the old wrong must die,
From pure gold all the dross will be burn'd, Time will
come they pro-claim from on high, When to
plowshares the sword shall be turn'd.

Chorus.
An-gels sing once a-gain, Oh, how sweet-ly they chant as of yore,

Angels Sing Once Again. Concluded.

3. We are glad that our Father in love,
Kindly grant that His children may know,
That our dear spirit friends from above,
Come to help make a heav'n here below.—Cho.

4. Then rejoice ever more, love shall reign,
Sing the sweet notes of joy once again,
Let all nations now join this refrain,
"Peace on earth and good will to all men."—Cho.

When We Arrive at Home.

1. Come sing for joy as we journey on our way,
Come sing for joy as we journey on our way,
Come sing for joy as we journey day by day,
   * For we are going home.
   Chorus.—Glory, glory, hallelujah! etc.

2. A bright angel band will meet us in the air,
A bright angel band will meet us in the air,
A bright angel band will meet us over there,
   And take our spirits home.—Cho.

3. Many are the mansions prepared for us above,
Many are the mansions prepared for us above,
Many are the mansions prepared by deeds of love,
   In that sweet summer home.—Cho.

4. How sweet it is to know that spirit friends are near,
How sweet it is to know that spirit friends are near,
How sweet it is to know that spirit friends are here,
   To cheer our journey home.—Cho.

5. They lift from our hearts the burdens that we bear,
They lift from our hearts the burdens that we bear,
They lift from our hearts the weary load of care,
   While on our journey home.—Cho.

6. All our worthy deeds are by angels written down,
All our worthy deeds are by angels written down,
All our worthy deeds will be jewels in our crown,
   When we arrive at home.—Cho.

* Repeat the last line of each verse for last line of Chorus.

Hymn of Peace and Progress.

B. M. L.
Moderato. cantabile.
GEO. BEAVERSON, by per.

1. Re-joice! and with the an-gels sing Glad tid-ings once a-gain,
2. The pure in heart with rapture hear Sweet seraphs from a-bove,

When right on earth will reign and bring Peace and good-will to men.
With words of hope and songs of cheer, Pro-claim the power of love.

Chorus.

Peace, Pro-gress, Light and Lib-er-ty! Come, chant the cheerful lay,

This truth in-deed will make thee free, And bring the joy-ful day.

3.
They come to prove man never dies,
  We only leave this clay;
When death shall come we only rise
  To everlasting day.

4.
There we shall have a just reward
  For all our words and deeds;
Our judge will be a righteous Lord,
  With no respect for creeds.

We Shall Meet Over There.

B. M. L. 　　　　　　　　　　　B. M. LAWRENCE, M. D.

1. We shall meet those we love o-ver there, In that pure, peaceful land of the blest,
When our hearts are all weighed down with care, This bright hope brings a sweet thought of rest.
2. We have mansions prepared for us there, Tho' like wan-der-ers here we may roam,
There the flow-ers are fade-less and fair, And the pil-grim at last finds a home.

Chorus.

We shall meet o-ver there, When the jour-ney of life here is o'er;
We shall meet o-ver there, We shall meet there to part nev-er more.

3
They have music most sweet over there,
And their harps are all brighter than gold,
Spotless white are the robes which they wear,
And the good there have treasures untold.

4
In that home for the soul over there,
All the motives of life will be known,
Then let each for that land now prepare,
Where all reap what on earth they have sown.

Open the Beautiful Gates for Me. Concluded.

5.
There is a place, a beautiful place,
Where they know not grief or care,
To gain that clime, that glorious clime,
We must lay up treasure there.

6.
That heav'n, that heav'n, that beautiful heav'n.
We may reach—not by one bound;
We build the ladder on which we rise,
And we climb up round by round.

Joyfully, Safe at Home.

1. Joyfully, joyfully onward we move,
   Bound for the land of the souls that we love;
   They can return, and they sing as they come,
   "Joyfully, joyfully thou shalt go home."

2. "Soon as thy life-work is ended on earth,
   Thou in the bright spirit-land shalt have birth;
   There with dear loved ones forever to roam,
   Joyfully, joyfully resting at home."

3. Friends we have loved who have passed on before,
   Now watch and wait as we draw near the shore;
   They come to banish from death all its gloom,
   Joyfully, joyfully will we go home.

4. Sweet angels' voices we all then shall hear,
   Celestial sonnets will fall on the ear;
   Those that we love there will sing as they come,
   "Joyfully, joyfully come to thy home."

5. "Death with his terror no more shall be King,
   Weapons of warfare will then loose their sting;
   Spirits who come from beyond the dark tomb,
   Joyfully, joyfully will lead thee home.

6. "Then while the years of eternity roll,
   Thou shalt rejoice in that rest for the soul;
   There where the storm-clouds of life never come
   Joyfully, joyfully safe, safe at home."

Oh, how Glorious!

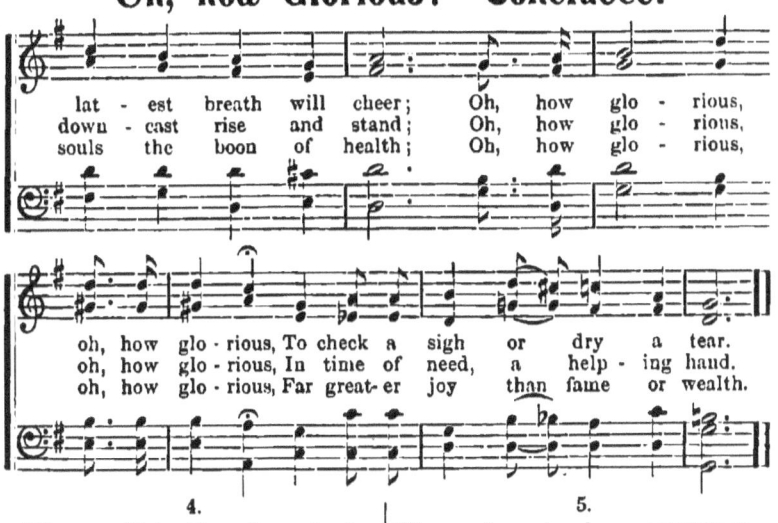

4.
When we think of homeless outcasts,
    Famishing for lack of food,
May we feel all men are brothers,
    And delight to do them good.
Oh, how glorious, oh, how glorious,
    When we remove another's woe;
Oh, how glorious, oh, how glorious,
    No sweeter joys the angels know.

5.
When we know loved ones are near us
    From the unseen world above,
Sordid aims and schemes will vanish,
    Then our souls will blend in love.
Oh, how glorious, oh, how glorious,
    This tho't will cheer our latest breath;
Oh, how glorious, oh, how glorious,
    When we shall triumph over death.

Sweet Hour of Pray'r.

1.
Sweet hour of pray'r! sweet hour of pray'r!
That calls us from a world of care,
And bids us at the Father's throne
Make all our wants and wishes known:
In seasons of distress and grief
Our souls can always find relief,
‖: And thus escape the tempter's snare,
By help from thee, sweet hour of pray'r! :‖

2.
Sweet hour of pray'r! sweet hour of pray'r!
Bring angels down from over there,
And may their tranquil truthfulness
Engage our waiting souls to bless:
May love divine bid passion cease,
And fill each soul with joy and peace,
‖: Let faith and hope remove despair,
Trusting in thee, sweet hour of pray'r! :‖

3.
Sweet hour of pray'r! sweet hour of pray'r!
May all mankind thy solace share
Until the Summer Land of light
To souls on earth shall come in sight;
And, when we drop this form and rise
To worlds of bliss, beyond the skies,
‖: May we, when free from earthly care,
Still cherish thee, sweet hour of pray'r! :‖

4.
With angels bright she went away,
Her home was in the skies;
Though now unseen, she lives to-day,
For true love never dies.
"At rest" we marked upon the stone
Above her grave so green,
"In heaven," she does not dwell alone,
But lives with "Angeline."

5.
And when my last day's work is done
Sweet Lulu's band will come,
In robes of splendor like the sun,
To bear my spirit home.
An angel now she comes to me
From life's immortal shore;
Her grave is green down by the sea,
But she lives ever more.

From the Other Shore.

"And He shall send His angels with a great sound of a trumpet."—MATT. xxiv: 31.

B. M. L. GEO. BEAVERSON, by per.

1. Through the port-als beam-ing, From a world of bliss,
2. Spir-its bright re-turn-ing, Pass-ing to and fro,

Gold-en light is stream-ing From that land to this.
Each have charge con-cern-ing, Dear one's left be-low.

Down to scenes ter-res-trial, Ser-aph's from a-bove,
They our feet are guard-ing Lest we dash a stone;

Chant-ing songs ce-les-tial, Come with hope and love.
No-ble deeds re-ward-ing, None are left a-lone.

From the Other Shore. Concluded.

3.
Few has earth of roses,
  Thorns and thistles grow;
Scarce we find oasis,
  Deserts burn below.
Here, 'mid gloom and sadness,
  We have toil and care;
But a world of gladness
  Waits us over there.

4.
In that blest to-morrow
  There is no more night;
And they know no sorrow
  In that land of light.
We shall pass the portals
  When for us they come;
And with dear immortals
  Find sweet rest at home

We shall Meet them Again. Concluded.

pub - lish these tid - ings a - far, How the grave to the good is the
- will from the soul-world of bliss, Where the loved ones still live, and our
meet them and know them a - gain; From the ev - er-green shore now they

gate - way to bliss, And the gates are now stand - ing a - jar.
hearts leap for joy, For that land has be-come one with this.
sing to us here: "Peace on earth, and good-will to all men!"

Chorus.

Oh, the sweet an - gel voi - ces we hear! Hark! the

love-tones are ring-ing o - ver there; And with joy now we gaze on the

spir - it form so dear, By the light from the oth - er land so fair.

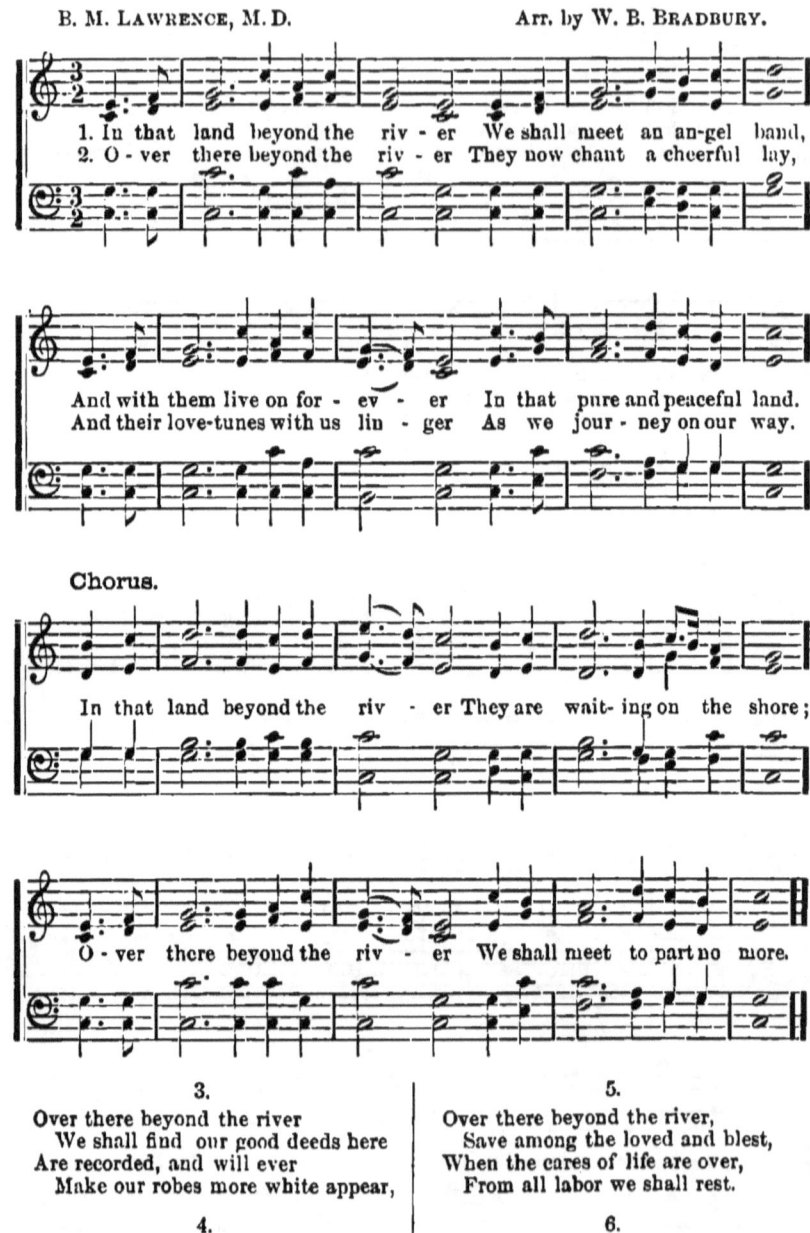

3.
Over there beyond the river
We shall find our good deeds here
Are recorded, and will ever
Make our robes more white appear,

4.
Over there beyond the river,
When our hearts are torn with grief,
Angels whisper they will never
Leave us when we need relief.

5.
Over there beyond the river,
Save among the loved and blest,
When the cares of life are over,
From all labor we shall rest.

6.
Over there beyond the river
We shall meet dear friends above,
And with them live on forever
In that peaceful land of love.

The Soul Has Fled.

Dr. B. M. Lawrence.

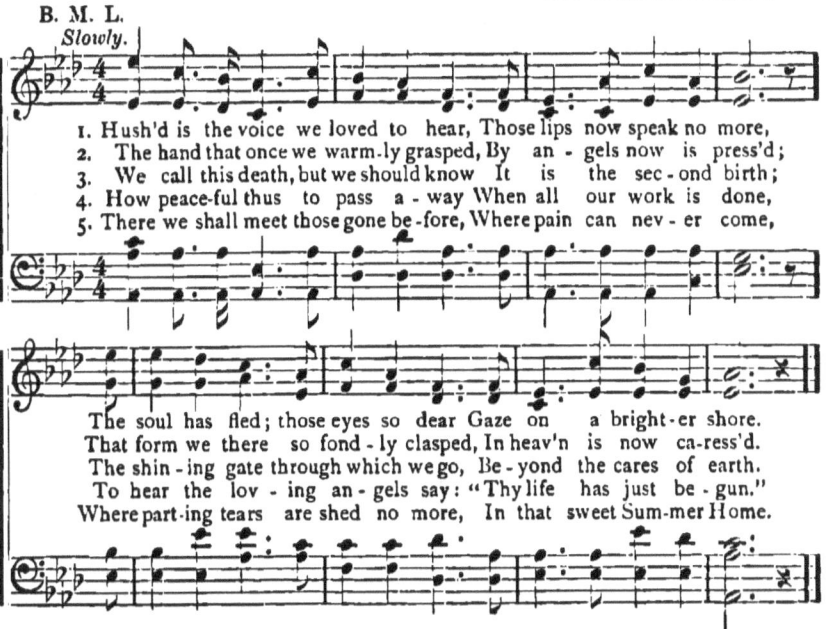

1. Hush'd is the voice we loved to hear, Those lips now speak no more,
The soul has fled; those eyes so dear Gaze on a bright-er shore.
2. The hand that once we warm-ly grasped, By an-gels now is press'd;
That form we there so fond-ly clasped, In heav'n is now ca-ress'd.
3. We call this death, but we should know It is the sec-ond birth;
The shin-ing gate through which we go, Be-yond the cares of earth.
4. How peace-ful thus to pass a-way When all our work is done,
To hear the lov-ing an-gels say: "Thy life has just be-gun."
5. There we shall meet those gone be-fore, Where pain can nev-er come,
Where part-ing tears are shed no more, In that sweet Sum-mer Home.

Waiting by the River.

Page 145, G. H.

Tune,— See opposite page.

1 We are waiting by the river,
   We are watching on the shore,
   Only waiting for the boatman
   In his bark to bear us o'er.

Chorus.—We are waiting, waiting, waiting,
   Watching, waiting on the shore,
   Only waiting, waiting, waiting
   Till the boatman bears us o'er.

2 While the mists hang o'er the river,
   And its billows loudly roar,
   We can hear celestal sonnets
   Wafted from the other shore.

3 Of that summer land of glory,
   We have caught such radiant gleams,
   Earth cannot compare in splendor
   With its peaceful vales and streams.

4 Over there are all the loved ones
   Who have faded from our side,
   With what joy we there shall meet them
   When we too shall cross the tide.

5 In that rest beyond the river,
   When we reach the other shore,
   We shall live with friends forever,
   Parting there will come no more.

Dora Bell's Pictures. Concluded.

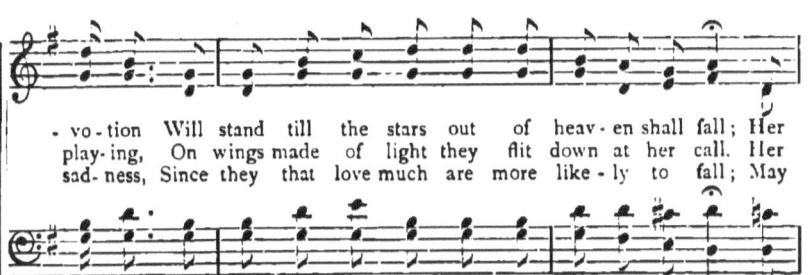

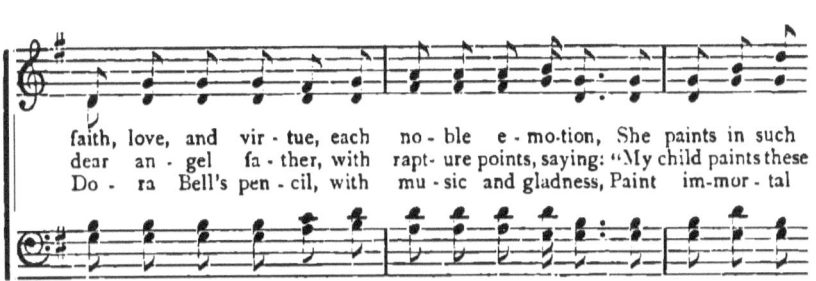

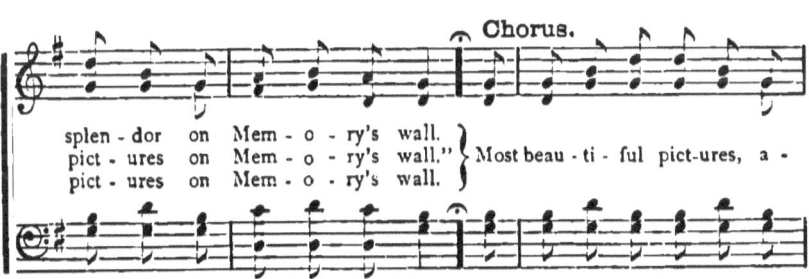

Wisdom Orders all Things Well.

"The first heaven and the first earth were passed away."—Rev. 21:1.

B. M. L.   Geo. Beaverson, by per.

1. When old wrong from earth shall per-ish, When old forms give place to new,
2. Crowns and thrones will have to crumble, Peace shall reign from shore to shore,
3. When mankind has learn'd this teaching, Wars and woes will sure-ly cease,

Men like an-gels then will cher-ish On-ly what proves just and true.
Right will then make old wrongs tumble, They shall fall to rise no more.
Then the world shall need no preaching, Love will fill all hearts with peace.

Thumb-worn creeds the truth repressing Will, like shad-ows, fade a-way;
Truth and might will wed to-geth-er; Joy-ful let this an-them swell;
Wis-dom from her shin-ing port-als Will prove all things work for good,

rit. pp

White-wing'd peace the whole earth blessing Then will bring the gold-en day.
"Peace on earth shall reign for-ev-er, Wis-dom or-ders all things well."
An-gels then will talk with mortals, And make earth one broth-er-hood.

We shall Gather at the River.

"A river the streams when of shall make glad.—Ps. 46: 4.

B. M. L.
GEO. BEAVERSON, by per.

1. We shall meet be-yond the riv - er, Where the bil - lows cease to roll;
2. Songs of those long gone before us Then will make our hearts re - joice;
3. We shall meet with all the lov'd ones, Torn on earth from our em-brace,
4. There throughout the end - less a - ges, Free from sor - row, pain or care,

There in all the bright for - ev - er Sor - row ne'er shall press the soul.
An - gels bright will swell the cho - rus With most sweet ce - les - tial voice.
We shall hear a - gain their voic - es, And be - hold them face to face.
We shall live with those that love us, There will be no part - ing there.

Chorus.

We shall gather by the riv - er, When our work on earth is o'er;
Yes we'll gather at the riv - er,

We shall gather by the riv - er, There to meet and part no more.
Yes we'll gather at the riv - er,

Waiting for the Morning. Concluded.

Chorus.
We are wait-ing, wait-ing, wait-ing While the long, long years increase;
We are wait-ing, wait-ing, wait-ing For the gold-en dawn of peace.

Sweet Spirits, can Return.

TUNE,—LENOX.   Page 119, G. H.

1. Proclaim the truth most clear
    To earth's remotest bound,
   Let all the nations hear
    The sweet, celestial sound,
   That spirits, from the unseen shore,
    Can now return to earth once more.

2. They come to banish care,
    To bid our sorrows cease,
   And prove that over there
    The pure shall rest in peace,
   With spirits, from the unseen shore,
    Who now return to earth once more.

3. With joyful notes they sing
    Sweet sonnets of the free,
   Since death has lost his sting,
    The grave its victory;
   While spirits, from the unseen shore,
    In love return to earth once more.

4. Beyond that golden gate,
    Where grief can never come,
   There loved ones for us wait,
    To bid us welcome home;
   Our spirits, from the unseen shore,
    Will then return to earth once more.

A Gentle, Kind Word. Concluded.

shad - ows of care de - part, And we feel in its gen - tle and
pride may the wound con - ceal, Re - mem - ber, the spir - it that is
the world may behold thee not, One gen - tle and kind ly word
ev - er thy fortune may fall, With a friend-ly smile, a free

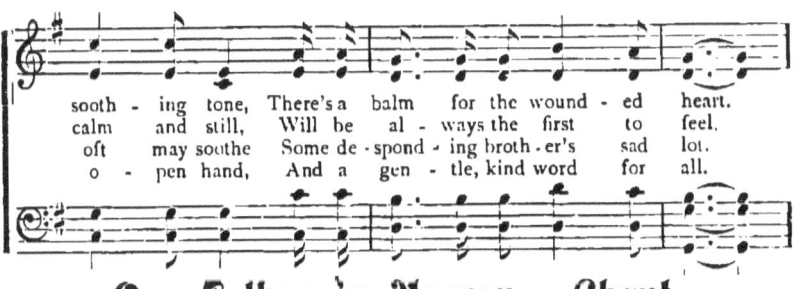

sooth - ing tone, There's a balm for the wound - ed heart.
calm and still, Will be al - ways the first to feel.
oft may soothe Some de - spond - ing broth - er's sad lot.
o - pen hand, And a gen - tle, kind word for all.

Our Father in Heaven. Chant.

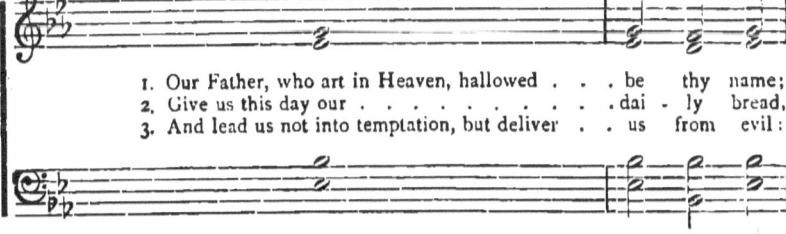

1. Our Father, who art in Heaven, hallowed . . . be thy name;
2. Give us this day our . . . . dai - ly bread,
3. And lead us not into temptation, but deliver . . us from evil:

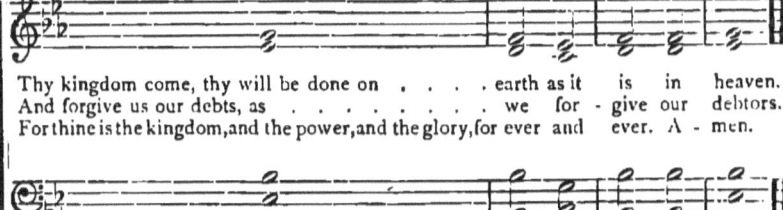

Thy kingdom come, thy will be done on . . . . earth as it is in heaven.
And forgive us our debts, as . . . . we for - give our debtors.
For thine is the kingdom, and the power, and the glory, for ever and ever. A - men.

Ocean Grove Declaration. Concluded.

thee, This world will be-come all a blank with-out thee.

4 Word, ocean, and grove,
Fail to tell all my love,
In spirit then, come, let us wander afar,
Where souls are divine,
And they know love like mine
||: Is pure as the light of a newly-born star. :||

5 True unions, sweet love,
Are all first made above,
In heaven my heart is pinioned to thine,
And angels to-day,
Will rejoice when you say,
:|| That henceforth thro' life will thy heart beat with mine. :||

A Beautiful World Above.

B. M. L.   Miss M. WALLACE.

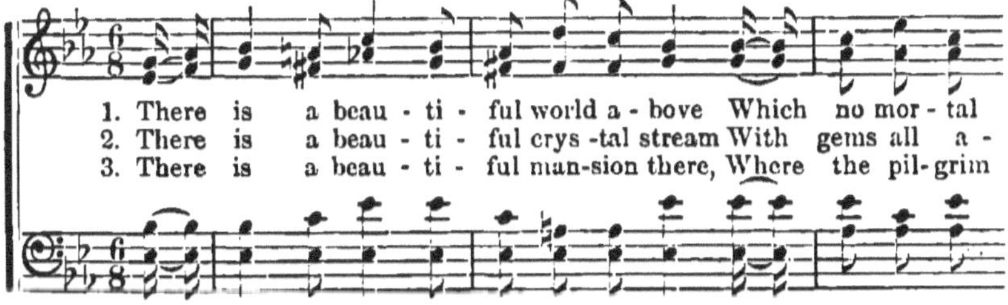

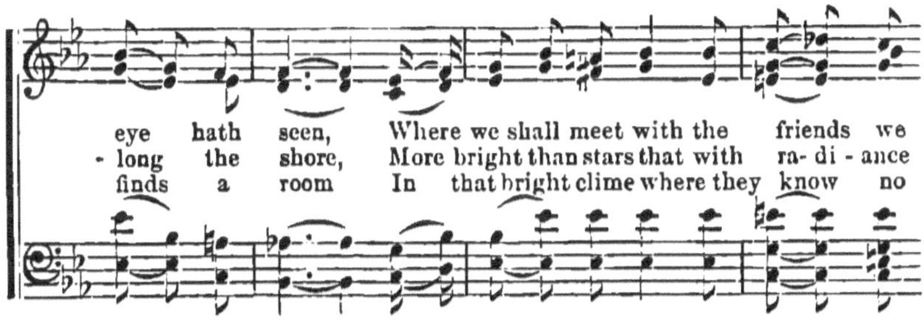

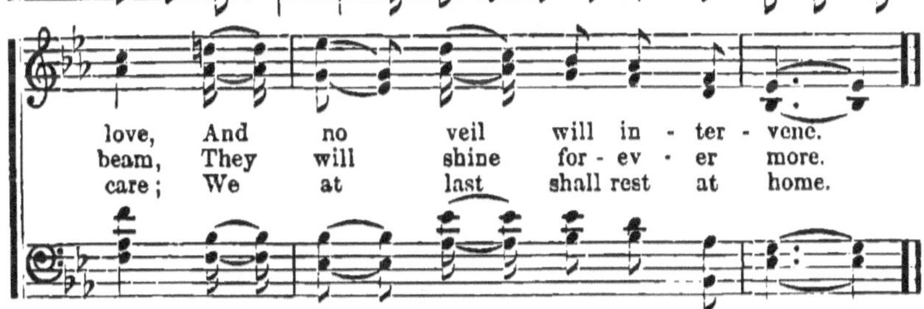

1. There is a beau-ti-ful world a-bove Which no mor-tal eye hath seen, Where we shall meet with the friends we love, And no veil will in-ter-vene.
2. There is a beau-ti-ful crys-tal stream With gems all a-long the shore, More bright than stars that with ra-di-ance beam, They will shine for-ev-er more.
3. There is a beau-ti-ful man-sion there, Where the pil-grim finds a room In that bright clime where they know no care; We at last shall rest at home.

4 There is a beautiful singing band,
With harps that are bright as gold,
They chant sweet sonnets in that far land
Where choristers ne'er seem old.

5 There in that beautiful world of light,
When our journey here is o'er,
With these we love all robed in pure white
We shall meet to part no more.

Dream Faces Celestial. Concluded.

Come, Dear Angel Guides.

"Are they not all ministering spirits."—HEB. 1: 14.

B. M. L.
B. M. LAWRENCE.

1. Come, dear an-gel-guides, draw near, Come and prove your presence here,
   Sweet-ly with our spir-its blend, Clos-er than an earth-ly friend;
   Shield us from the cares of life, And from sor-did scenes of strife.

2. Come, bright an-gels, from on high, Prove that love can nev-er die;
   May that pearl of great-est price Make this earth a par-a-dise;
   Rent the veil, which o-ver there Hides from view that world so fair.

Chorus.

Guard and guide us to that shore, Where the storm-clouds come no more;
Guard and guide us to that shore, Where the storm-clouds come no more.

3 Come and lead us in the light,
  Make our pathway smooth and bright,
  When dark trials meet us here;
  May the star of hope shine clear,
  Leading us to that fair clime,
  Free from all the cares of time.

4 When we breathe our latest breath,
  Come and quell all fears of death,
  Then beyond the silent tomb,
  Where the fadeless flowers bloom,
  May we on that peaceful shore
  Meet our friends and part no more.

3 From the sweat of their brows the deserts bloom,
  And the forest before them falls;
  Their labor has builded humble homes,
  And the palace with stately halls.
  But the rumseller owns both homes and lands,
  While the ninety and nine have empty hands.

4 But the night so dreary, so dark, so long,
  At last shall the bright morning bring,
  And over the land the temp'rance song
  Of the ninety and nine shall ring,
  And echo afar, from shore to shore:
  Rejoice! the rum fiend shall reign no more!

4 Angels know our way is dreary
While on our journey home;
And they know our feet grow weary
While on our journey home.

5 But beyond the storm to-morrow
We shall arrive at home,
Then farewell to grief and sorrow
When we arrive at home.

Wisdom Better than Gold. Concluded.

The Pilgrim's Daily Prayer.

B. M. LAWRENCE. GEO. BEAVERSON, by per.

1. Thou source of Life, oh, hear my pray'r, For guidance thro' each day;
2. Thou source of Light, oh, hear my pray'r, Send sunshine to my soul;
3. Thou source of Love, oh, hear my pray'r, Let me not live in vain;

May Thy pure guarding an-gels keep My feet in wisdom's way.
Be Thou my guide on life's dark sea When bil-lows round me roll.
Teach me to place more trust in Thee, Make all my du-ties plain.

Chorus.

Hear my pray'r, oh, hear my pray'r, Guard and keep me in Thy care;

Lov-ing Fa-ther, hear my pray'r, Hear, oh, hear my heartfelt pray'r!

4 Thou source of Truth, oh, hear my prayer,
That all mankind may know
Our loved ones can return to earth,
And bring sweet heaven below.—CHO.

5 Thou source of Wisdom, hear my prayer,
That, while on earth I roam,
Bright angels may my course control,
And guide me safely home.—CHO.

Sweet Summer-Land.—Concluded.

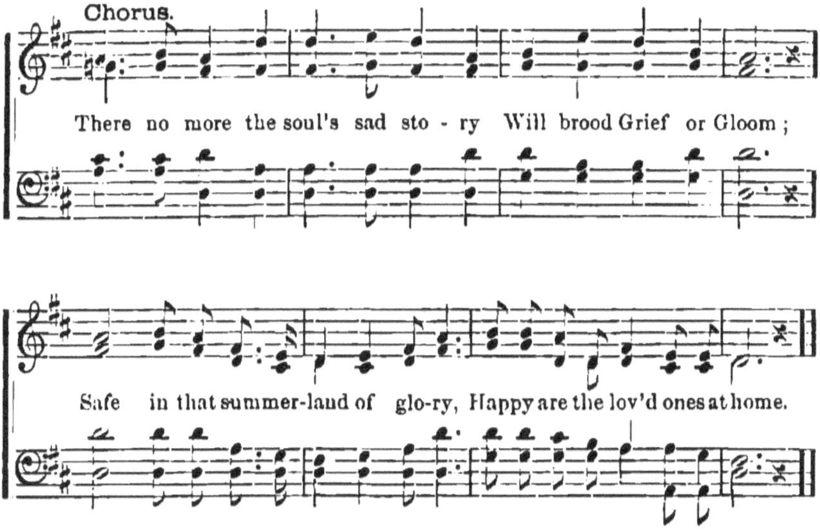

Chorus.

There no more the soul's sad sto-ry Will brood Grief or Gloom;
Safe in that summer-land of glo-ry, Happy are the lov'd ones at home.

Aspiration of Purity and Love.

B. M. L. B. M. LAWRENCE, M. D.

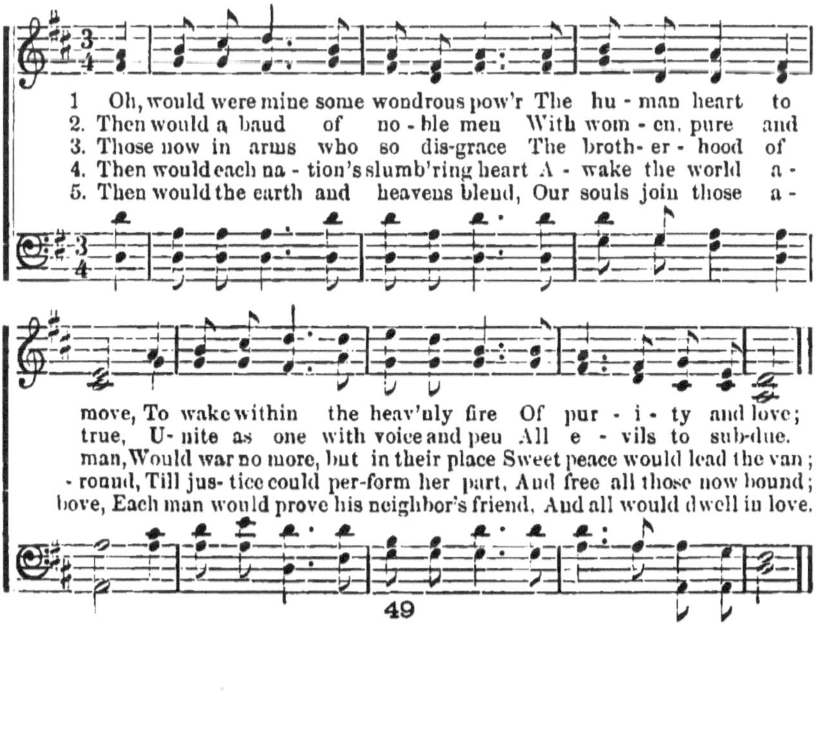

1. Oh, would were mine some wondrous pow'r The hu-man heart to
2. Then would a band of no-ble men With wom-en, pure and
3. Those now in arms who so dis-grace The broth-er-hood of
4. Then would each na-tion's slumb'ring heart A-wake the world a-
5. Then would the earth and heavens blend, Our souls join those a-

move, To wake within the heav'nly fire Of pur-i-ty and love;
true, U-nite as one with voice and pen All e-vils to sub-due.
man, Would war no more, but in their place Sweet peace would lead the van;
-round, Till jus-tice could per-form her part, And free all those now bound;
bove, Each man would prove his neighbor's friend, And all would dwell in love.

The Cross Wins the Crown.

"Ye must be born again."—JOHN 3: 7.

B. M. L. B. M. LAWRENCE, M. D.

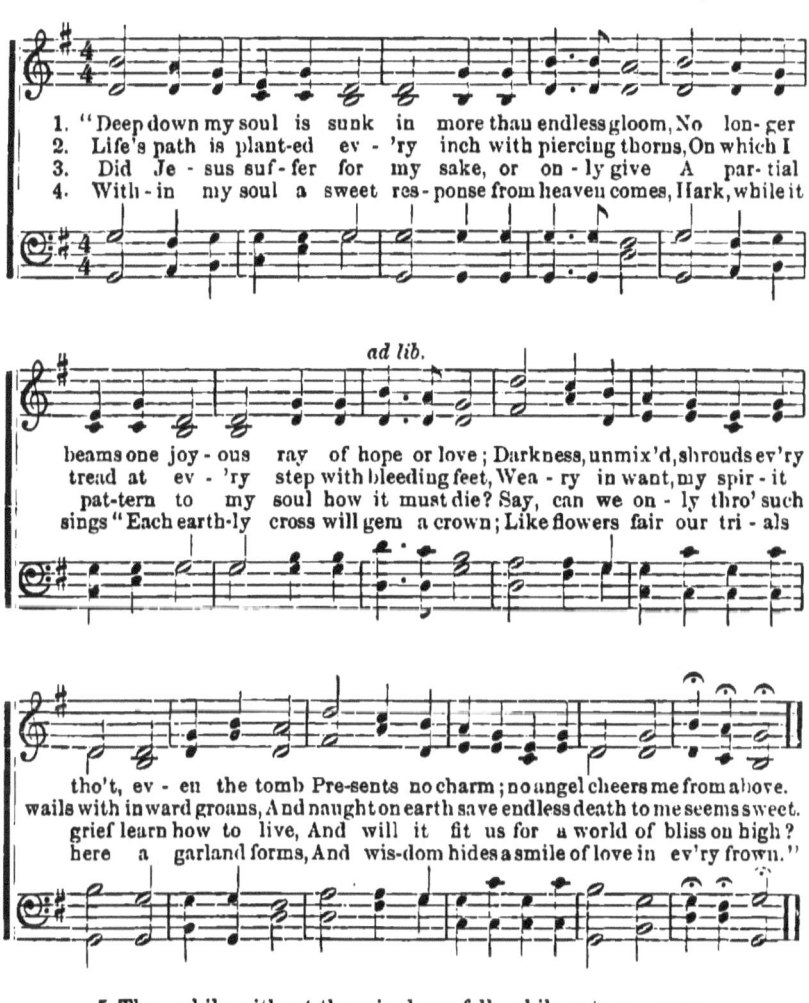

1. "Deep down my soul is sunk in more than endless gloom, No longer beams one joyous ray of hope or love; Darkness, unmix'd, shrouds ev'ry tho't, ev-en the tomb Presents no charm; no angel cheers me from above.
2. Life's path is plant-ed ev-'ry inch with piercing thorns, On which I tread at ev-'ry step with bleeding feet, Wea-ry in want, my spir-it wails with inward groans, And naught on earth save endless death to me seems sweet.
3. Did Je-sus suf-fer for my sake, or on-ly give A par-tial pat-tern to my soul how it must die? Say, can we on-ly thro' such grief learn how to live, And will it fit us for a world of bliss on high?
4. With-in my soul a sweet res-ponse from heaven comes, Hark, while it sings "Each earth-ly cross will gem a crown; Like flowers fair our tri-als here a garland forms, And wis-dom hides a smile of love in ev'ry frown."

5 Then while without the rain drops fall, while nature weeps,
   Within my soul the storm has broke, the bow appears,
And joy like laughing rills through all my being leaps,
   Tears are but dew—a holy calm quells all my fears.

6 Trust, doubting soul, the unseen power that rules o'er all,
   Is not thy life of greater worth than lilies bloom?
Behold His loving hand who check the sparrows' fall,
   And from this moment banish all thy faithless gloom.

Alcohol; or, the Pirate Prince.

B. M. L. Dr. B. M. LAWRENCE.

1. "Oh, I command a dreadful band Of Pirates, seared with crimes,
They worship me on land and sea, And sing my praise in rhymes;
Laws for my sake they frame or break, My kingdom has no end;
In ev-'ry land, up-on each hand, The rulers call me friend.

2. "I love to sail in a wrecking gale With a wild and wicked crew,
My flag, blood-red, hung at mast-head, Rich prizes plain in view;
With songs and cheers my pilot steers Straight for the souls of men,
One conquest o'er we long for more, And hoist our sails a-gain.

Alcohol; or, the Pirate Prince.—Concluded.

"Oh, millions of slaves I send to graves, Yes, millions of slaves to pauper's graves;
Chorus for last verse.
In oblivion deep may they ever sleep, In oblivion deep may the whole crew sleep,

"The fair-est be-fore me fall; Now a se-cret let me tell:
The Rum-trade robbers one and all, For we all know now full well

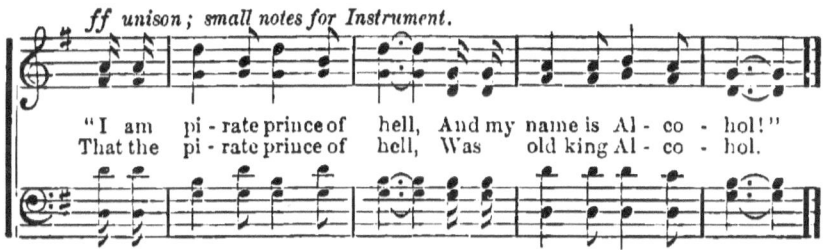

"I am pi-rate prince of hell, And my name is Al-co-hol!"
That the pi-rate prince of hell, Was old king Al-co-hol.

3 " Sons, brave and true, fair daughters, too,
    For me with hatred burn,
  They sing and pray that soon I may
    Set sail and ne'er return ;
  But until they vote as they pray,
    At all their schemes I smile,
  Their sons I'll kill, their land I'll fill
    With crime, war, want, and guile."

4 A ship of might has hove in sight,
    A model craft from Maine,
  Her deadly shot comes fast and hot,
    Nor is one fired in vain ;
  The pirate horde with all on board
    Fight fiend-like for their crown,
  Till a ballet-ball strikes Alcohol,
    Then, crew, and ship go down.

Learn to do Well.—Concluded.

one's self or na-tion That can e-qual this plan.
se-quence of ac-tions, Both of bod-y and mind.
keep ev-er near thee, Help-ing thee to win fame.

Chorus.
Oh, then learn, ... oh, learn to do well, ...
Oh, then learn, oh, learn to do well, to do well,

Do the best, ... the best that you can,
Do the best, the best that you can, do the best;

Not e-ven an an-gel from heav-en could tell A-ny

way of sal-vation for one's self or na-tion That can e-quel this plan.

The Dying Mother's Request.

B. M. L.　　　　　　　　　　　　　　　　　　　　B. M. LAWRENCE.

1. "My dar-ling boy," his moth-er cried, "Come, hear my last re-quest
2. "Your fath-er once was good and true, A hap-py home was mine,
3. "Re-member, boy, 'twas rum that dealt The fa-tal, dead-ly blow;
4. "O, mother, dear, your boy, tho' young, Has learned to hate the bowl,

Be-fore my spir-it takes its flight, And this sad heart finds rest;
But, when the cru-el tempt-er came He fell by drink-ing wine.
It nerved the hand that did the deed Which made the life-blood flow.
The curs-ed cup which fa-ther drank, That stained his priceless soul.

But, ere I leave this world of woe, Oh, heed my dy-ing call:
Think what a wreck my life has been Made by your fa-ther's fall;
Strong drink has made my life a blank; This hope re-mains, that all
But, mother, dear, I pledge you here Be-fore the God of all:

And pledge to fight, while life shall last, The de-mon, Al-co-hol!
Then pledge to war, while strength shall last, The de-mon, Al-co-hol!
Thro' life you'll fight, with all your might, The de-mon, Al-co-hol!"
Thro' life to fight, with all my might, The de-mon, Al-co-hol!"

A Nation Born Again.

TUNE.—See opposite page.

1 He gazed upon the gathered throng,
   The scaffold standing near,
  Then with a prophet's voice he spoke,
   For all the world to hear:
  "In Freedom's name 'tis sweet to die;
   Mark this, my countrymen:
  Erin by martyrs must become
   A nation born again.

2 "Let no man write my epitaph,
   Until my country stands
  Among the nations of the earth
   The freest of free lands.
  When Irishmen shall all unite,
   Despot's may rage in vain;
  Erin at once will then become
   A nation born again."

3 Around young Emmet's grave each
   A mighty host appears;   [year
  Garlands above the sod they weave,
   And shed for him their tears.
  A costly stone shall mark the place
   Where long his dust has lain,
  Soon as his native land becomes
   A nation born again.

4 A truer man ne'er trod the earth,
   No human heart more brave;
  His fame shall last while Freedom
   With those he died to save. [dwells
  Emmet still lives—Truth never dies,
   Gallows are built in vain;
  And with his monument shall rise
   A nation born again.

B. M. L.

The Temperance Banner.

2 Come, join the noble army,
   Enlist now for the fight;
  Maintain our nation's honor,
   Firm stand ye for the right.
  Promote the cause of Temperance,
   To aid poor fallen man;
  Put on the glorious armor,
   Be foremost in the van.

3 Then rally round the standard,
   And let the work go on
  Until the last dim vestige
   Of intemperance is gone.
  Be earnest in the battle,
   Your weapons boldly wield;
  You'll surely gain the victory,
   And make the monster yield.

All Hail the Time.—Concluded.

The Glory Thine.

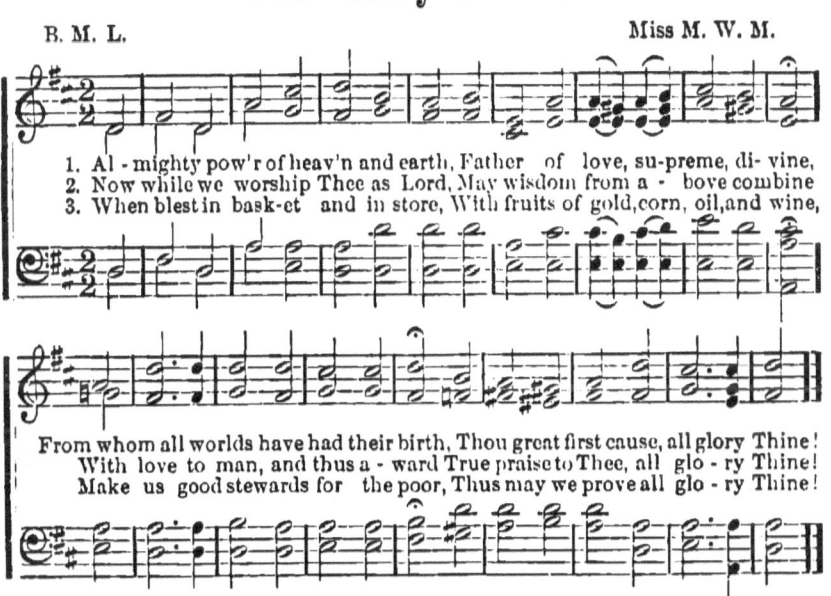

4 When disappointments cloud our way,
　Grant that our souls may not repine,
　But may we see in life's dark day
　Beyond the clouds, all glory Thine!

5 Let angels, from the unseen shore,
　Now fill our hearts with love divine;
　And may we feel forever more
　Thy will be done, all glory Thine.

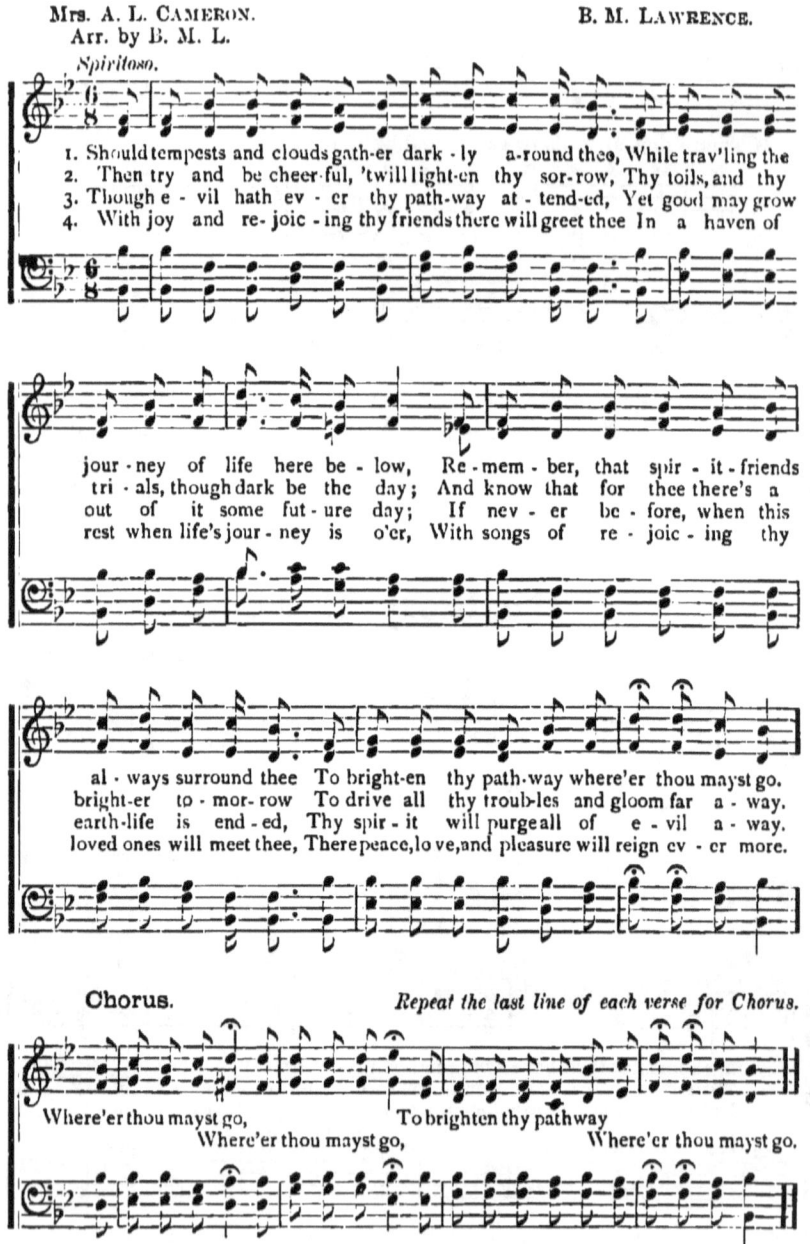

The Ship of Life.

"Which hope we have as an anchor."—Heb: 6: 19.

B. M. L. GEO. BEAVERSON, by per.

1. Our ship glides o'er the wa - ter, With col - ors flow-ing free, Bound for a fair - er quar - ter, We're sail-ing on life's sea.
2. With pro - gress for our com - pass, Which ev - er points a - bove, And pray'r that heav'n may guide us, We'll gain the port of love.

Chorus.

Oh, hear sweet voi - ces sing - ing, Songs from the oth - er shore; Peace an - gels now are bring - ing Good will on earth once more.

3 With wisdom for our captain,
　Love-mates our loyal crew,
　Faith is our trusty watchman,
　And hope our beacon true.—CHO.

4 Souls gone before still hover
　Round us on wings of love,
　While we are sailing over
　They lift our thoughts above.—CHO.

5 When passion storms have bound us,
　Peace comes to quell the blest;
　When breakers bleak surround us,
　Hope will her anchor cast.—CHO.

6 With angel friends beside us,
　All sordid aims will cease,
　Our pilot, prayer, will guide us
　Safe in the port of peace.—CHO.

"Back-Bone." Etc.—Concluded.

Drink Wine no More!

"Abstain from all appearance of evil."—1 THES. 5: 22.

G. H. No. 83.　　　　　　　　　　　　　　　　B. M. L.

1 Wine is a mocker, brother, all through the land,
Thousands are falling by the drink-maker's hand;
Dark is the drunkard's future, woes are in store,
Sign the pledge, then be a man, and drink wine no more.

CHORUS.—Drink wine no more, brother, drink wine no more,
　　Heed not the tempter's voice, but pass by his door;
　　Dram shops have ruined, brother, many thousand score;
　　Shun the road that leads to death, and drink wine no more.

2 Trust in the temperance banner, it will not fail;
Rum shall not always rule; the right must prevail;
Heed not the morbid thirst, each appetite control,
Ever let this be thy watchword: "Drink blights the soul!"—CHO.

3 Work for the morning, brother, that time will come
When nations shall forever stop making rum,
Then we shall sing, as we never sang before:
"Glory, glory hallelujah! Rum rules no more!"—CHO.

The Golden Years to Come.—Concluded.

The Grand Era, Etc.—Concluded.

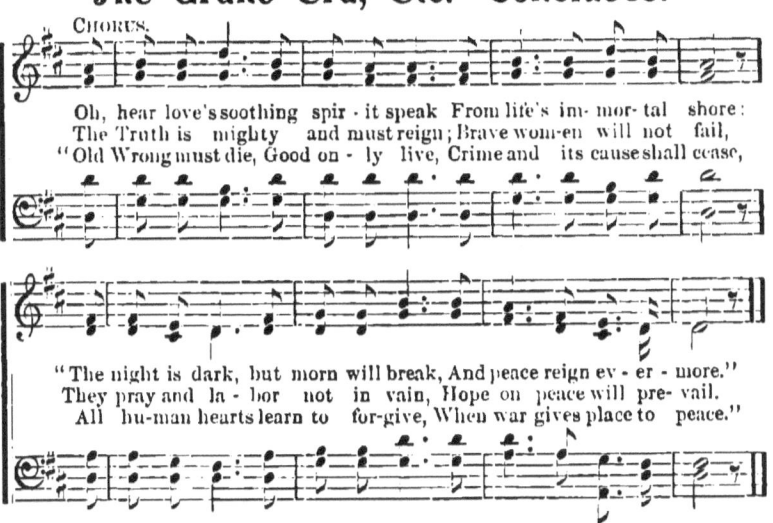

CHORUS.

Oh, hear love's soothing spir-it speak From life's im-mor-tal shore:
The Truth is mighty and must reign; Brave wom-en will not fail,
"Old Wrong must die, Good on-ly live, Crime and its cause shall cease,

"The night is dark, but morn will break, And peace reign ev-er-more."
They pray and la-bor not in vain, Hope on peace will pre-vail.
All hu-man hearts learn to for-give, When war gives place to peace."

Prophet, Tell Us of the Light.

B. M. L.   B. M. LAWRENCE.

1. Prophet, tell us of the light, What its signs of promise are. Pil-grim, o'er yon mountain's height, See that glo-ry-beam-ing star, See that glo-ry-beam-ing star.

2 Prophet, tell us of the light,
   Higher yet that star ascends.
Pilgrim, virtue, truth, and right,
   Love and peace, its course portends.

3 Prophet, tell us of the light,
   For the morning seems to dawn.
Pilgrim, darkness takes its flight,
   Doubt and terror are withdrawn.

4 Prophet, will its beams alone
   Gild the spot that gave them birth?
Pilgrim, ages, yet unknown,
   It will shine o'er all the earth.

5 Prophet, will the rule of wrong
   And injustice soon be o'er?
Pilgrim, angels sing their song:
   "Peace shall reign forever more!"

Dare to be Free.—Concluded.

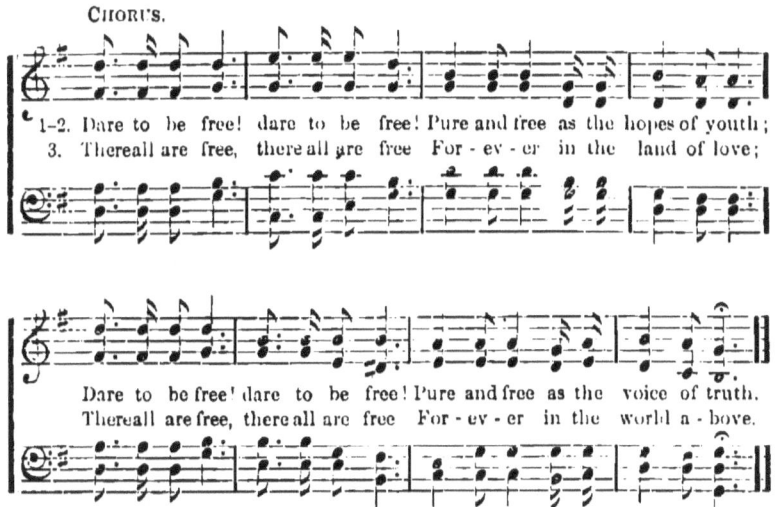

1-2. Dare to be free! dare to be free! Pure and free as the hopes of youth;
3. There all are free, there all are free For-ev-er in the land of love;

Dare to be free! dare to be free! Pure and free as the voice of truth.
There all are free, there all are free For-ev-er in the world a-bove.

Peace Beyond the River.

"To keep thee in all thy ways."—PSA. 91: 11.

G. H. No. 45. B. M. LAWRENCE.

1 Angels, keep me in the light
Shining from truth's mountain,
Where the loving streams are bright,
Flowing from love's fountain.

CHORUS.—In the light, in the light,
Angels, keep me ever,
Till the soul at last shall find
Peace beyond the river.

2 Blind with creeds, from ages past,
Loving spirits found me,
Like a morning star they cast
Light and hope around me.—CHO.

3 Now they guard me day and night,
Kindly watching o'er me;
And they lead me in the light,
With bright scenes before me.—CHO.

4 With a firm and faithful hand
They will guide me ever,
Till I reach the summer land,
Over death's dark river.—CHO.

5 There where all is peace and light,
Friends no more shall sever,
But with loved ones, robed in white,
Still live on forever.—CHO.

Tell Me Not I'm Growing Old.

"The years of thy life shall be increased.—PROV. 9: 11."

B. M. L.　　　　　　　　　　　　　　　　B. M. LAWRENCE.

1. Tell me not that youth is fleet-ing While the heart beats full and strong;
2. Growing old! my faith and feel-ings Each are firm and act-ive still;
3. Mirth, once merry at my com-ing, Now is hushed or whispers low;
4. Far a-cross the peace-ful riv-er, Dreaded so in days of yore,

Never felt the soul more man-ful, Nor so full of love and song;
Nerves are sound, and eyes clear see-ing, Tho'ts and brain o-bey the will.
When I pause and lin-ger near them, Streams of bliss run soft and slow.
Ma-ny pre-cious friends and kin-dred Wait for me be-yond the shore;

Earth-life ne'er seem'd more worth liv-ing, Ev-'ry day new hopes un-fold;
On-ly from the fad-ing tem-ples, And the fur-rows Time has told,
Tho' I prize the joys of childhood, And of youth more than fine gold,
When my time shall come to join them, Where life's record is un-roll'd,

And they sure-ly must be dream-ing Those who think I'm growing old.
Does the flight of youth seem re-al, Show-ing that I'm grow-ing old.
Sometimes now they seem to shun me, For they think I'm growing old.
Welcome then will be the greeting: "Come, where love will ne'er grow old!"

Summer Sweet, Etc.—Concluded.

That be-yond the si-lent tomb Summer sweet a-gain shall bloom;
When be-yond the si-lent tomb Summer sweet a-gain shall bloom;
There be-yond the peaceful tomb Summer shall for-ev-er bloom;

Shall ev-er bloom, shall ev-er bloom;
Shall ev-er bloom......... shall ev-er bloom;

Yes, be-yond the si-lent tomb Summer sweet shall ev-er bloom.

Angel Guide, I Need Thee.

"He shall give His angels charge over thee."—PSA. 91: 11.

G. H. No. 3.   B. M. L.

1 I need Thee every hour,
   Dear Angel Guide,
  Come with Thy soothing power,
   Keep near my side.

CHO.—I need Thee, oh! I need Thee
     Gently to guard and lead me,
     Every hour I need Thee,
     Oh, come to me.

2 I need Thee every hour,
   Come from above,
  Guide me in wisdom's ways,
   With peace and love.—CHO.

3 I need Thee every hour
   While traveling here;
  Temptations lose their power
   When Thou art near.—CHO.

4 I need Thee every hour,
   Still nearer come;
  Let me not from Thee stray
   Till safe at home.—CHO.

5 I need Thee every hour;
   When life is o'er
  Then may we meet above,
   And part no more.—CHO.

There is Room among the Angels.

"For of such is the kingdom of heaven."—Matt. 19: 14.

Anon.
Geo. Beaverson.

Affettuoso.

1. There is room a-mong the an-gels For the spir-it of your child;
2. "I have sore-ly tried you, mother, Been to you a con-stant care,
3. "I was not so wayward, mother, Not so ver-y, ver-y bad,

They will take your lit-tle Ma-ry In their lov-ing arms so mild;
And you will not miss me, mother, When I dwell a-mong the fair;
But what ten-der love would nourish, And make Ma-ry's heart so glad;

They will ev-er love her fond-ly, As the sto-ry books have said;
For you have no room for Ma-ry, She was ev-er in your way,
Oh, I yearn'd for pure af-fec-tion In this world of bit-ter woe;

They will find a home for Ma-ry,—Ma-ry numbered with the dead.
And she fears the good will shun her; Will they, darling moth-er, say?
And I long for bliss immor-tal In that land where I must go.

["The mother struck the child a severe blow, saying, with anger, that she was always in the way. Two weeks after, on her death-bed, while delirious, she said, "I was always in your way, mother, you had no room for little Mary! And will I be in the angels' way?" The broken-hearted mother then felt no sacrifice too great, could she have saved her child.]

There is Room, Etc.—Concluded.

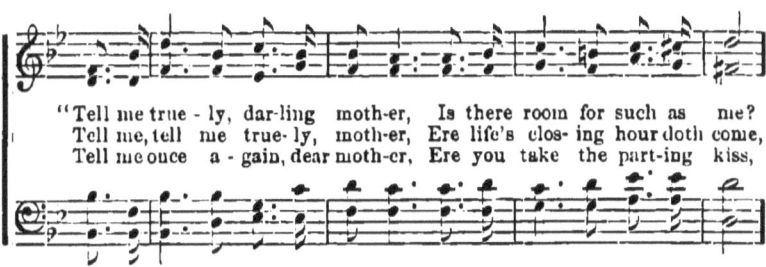

"Tell me true-ly, dar-ling moth-er, Is there room for such as me?
Tell me, tell me true-ly, moth-er, Ere life's clos-ing hour doth come,
Tell me once a-gain, dear moth-er, Ere you take the part-ing kiss,

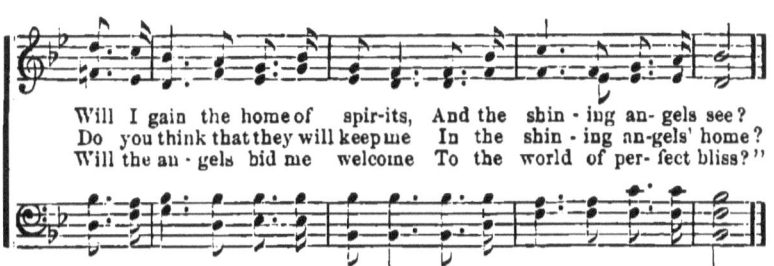

Will I gain the home of spir-its, And the shin-ing an-gels see?
Do you think that they will keep me In the shin-ing an-gels' home?
Will the an-gels bid me welcome To the world of per-fect bliss?"

Come Hear the Welcome Voice!

"The truth shall make you free,"—JOHN 8: 23.

G. H. No. 63.   B. M. L.

1 Come hear the welcome voice
   That calls thee from above,
   It bids thee, while on earth to live,
   A life of truth and love.

CHO.—Hear the angel voice
   Calling unto thee;
   Hark! it bids thy soul rejoice
   From fears of death made free.

2 It sings: "there is no death,"
   That loved ones can return,
   They are not lost; forever gone
   To some far distant bourne.

3 They now are angels bright,
   Sent forth to guide thy feet,
   In love they come, enrobed in white,
   Their friends on earth to greet.

4 They say: "thou shalt receive
   Reward for all thy deeds!"
   In that fair land, of light and peace,
   They have no forms and creeds.

5 There truth alone will make
   The spirit light and free,
   And kindly deeds, in heaven's court,
   Will need no other plea.

6 Then hail the voice of truth,
   For angels sing again:
   "The dawn of peace thro'out the earth,
   And good-will to all men!"

Lead me, Loving Angels.

"Prayer of the righteous man availeth much."—Jas. 5: 16.

B. M. L. B. M. LAWRENCE.

2 Teach us that our strength is weakness
  When compared with Thine,
  And although to err is human,
  To forgive's divine.—CHO.

3 May we each become less selfish
  When our souls are grown,
  We shall feel a brother's welfare
  Equal with our own.—CHO.

4 Earth will then become like heaven;
  Wrong will reign no more;
  Men will walk and talk with angels
  From the other shore.—CHO.

5 Father, we are weary pilgrims,
  Plodding on our way,
  And we pray that guarding angels
  Guide our feet each day.—CHO.

The Golden Day is Dawning.—Concluded.

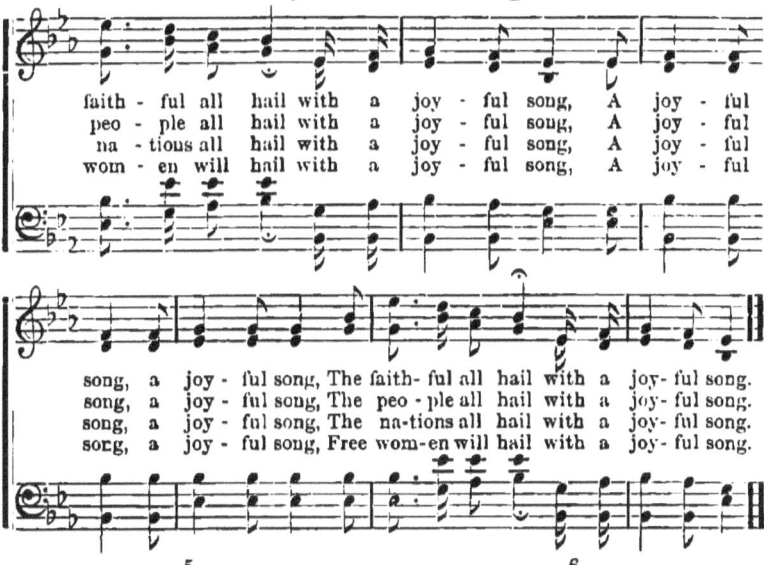

faith - ful all hail with a joy - ful song, A joy - ful
peo - ple all hail with a joy - ful song, A joy - ful
na - tions all hail with a joy - ful song, A joy - ful
wom - en will hail with a joy - ful song, A joy - ful

song, a joy - ful song, The faith- ful all hail with a joy- ful song.
song, a joy - ful song, The peo - ple all hail with a joy- ful song.
song, a joy - ful song, The na-tions all hail with a joy- ful song.
song, a joy - ful song, Free wom-en will hail with a joy- ful song.

5.
Then in that golden time coming,
  When right is might, and all made free,
The earth more bright than Eden bloom-
  Will swell with songs of liberty. [ing
Then the new era they've toiled for so long,
The toilers all hail with a joyful song,
  A joyful song, a joyful song,
The toilers all hail with a joyful song.

6.
The hosts of heaven and earth combin-
  ing,
Will carry on the work begun;
The star of hope within us shining,
  Proclaims the victory well nigh won.
Then the new era, they've hoped for so long,
The angels will hail with a joyful song,
  A joyful song, a joyful song,
The angels all hail with a joyful song.

Over on the Other Shore.

"Comfort one another with these words."—1 THES. 4: 18.

G. H. No. 72.   B. M. L.

1 Angel friends now hover near us,
    As we journey to and fro;
  When we call they always hear us,
    Wheresoe'er on earth we go.

Cho.—Precious thought! oh, how sweet
    Over on the other shore;
  Precious thought! oh, how sweet;
    We shall meet to part no more.

2 We shall cross the silent river,
    When they call for us to come,

  And with friends live on forever,
    In the soul's bright summer home.
                                    CHO.
3 Precious thought! we all are going
    To a world of peace and joy.
  There to reap reward for sowing
    Truth and love without alloy.—CHO.

4 Oh, the precious thought of seeing
    Those we love now gone before,
  And while time shall last, of being
    Safe with them for ever more.—CHO.

That Evergreen Shore.—Concluded.

ev-er-green shore. There we shall be free for-ev-
-er to roam, Where sor-row will come no more.

Doxologies.

Tune.—OLD HUNDRED. L. BOURGEOIS.

No. 1. Praise God, from whom all blessings flow; Praise Him, by soothing grief and woe;
Praise Him, as angels praise above; Praise Him, with wisdom, truth, and love.

2. Thou Great first-cause, supreme, most high,
Whose glory fills the earth and sky,
May Thy love make us more divine,
Till we become most truly Thine.

3. Source of all light, to Thee we pray
While passing through life's darkest day,
For clearer sight that we may see
The path that leads more near to Thee.

4. Thou God of Peace, before we part,
Send some kind angel to each heart,
Lead us, we pray, with loving hand
Until we reach the Summer Land.

5. Dear angel-guides, may thy sweet peace
Remain with us till life shall cease,
Then bear our souls to that bright shore
Where loved ones meet to part no more.

The Plowshares of Peace.—Concluded.

All the world shall bow to la-bor; Strikes and boy-cotts cease;
When the world shall bow to la-bor; Strikes and boy-cotts cease;
Soon the world shall bow to la-bor; Strikes and boy-cotts cease;
When the world shall bow to la-bor; Strikes and boy-cotts cease;

Wars come no more; the spear and sabre Shall become the plowshares of peace.

Green Isle of the Ocean.

"The land shall not be sold for ever; for the land is mine."—LEV. 25: 23.

Air: "The Red, White, and Blue." B. M. L.

1.

All hail thou green isle of the ocean,
  Thy martyrs are making thee free;
Other lands may admire thy devotion,
  But Columbia sends greeting to thee.
Since the day when her great Declaration
  Thrill'd the hearts of all people oppress'd,
She has longed to behold thee a nation:
  The grandest, the freest, the best.

2.

Must the few rob the many forever,
  And reap what their brothers have sown?
The voice of the people shout: No, never!
  Henceforth men must earn what they own.
Britain's minions may force more evictions,
  But brave men now make this demand:
Once again hear the prophet's predictions,
  God's children must all own His land.

3.

Were the lives of the heroes all written,
  Who fought with the great Washington,
We would find Erin conquered Bull-Britain,
  By her independence was won.
Irish women took part in the struggle,
  And filled up the ranks where men fell;
Molly Pitcher was made of such metal
  As the mother and daughters—Parnell.

4.

Then, hail thou, green isle of the ocean,
  United thy sons shall prevail;
Manifesto ne'er made such commotion,
  As thine from the Kilmainham jail.
Then three cheers for the young hero Emmet,
  And three for the land loved so well,
Three times three for the brave Michael Davitt,
  And three more for the gallant Parnell.

Set thy House in Order.

B. M. L.
B. M. LAWRENCE.

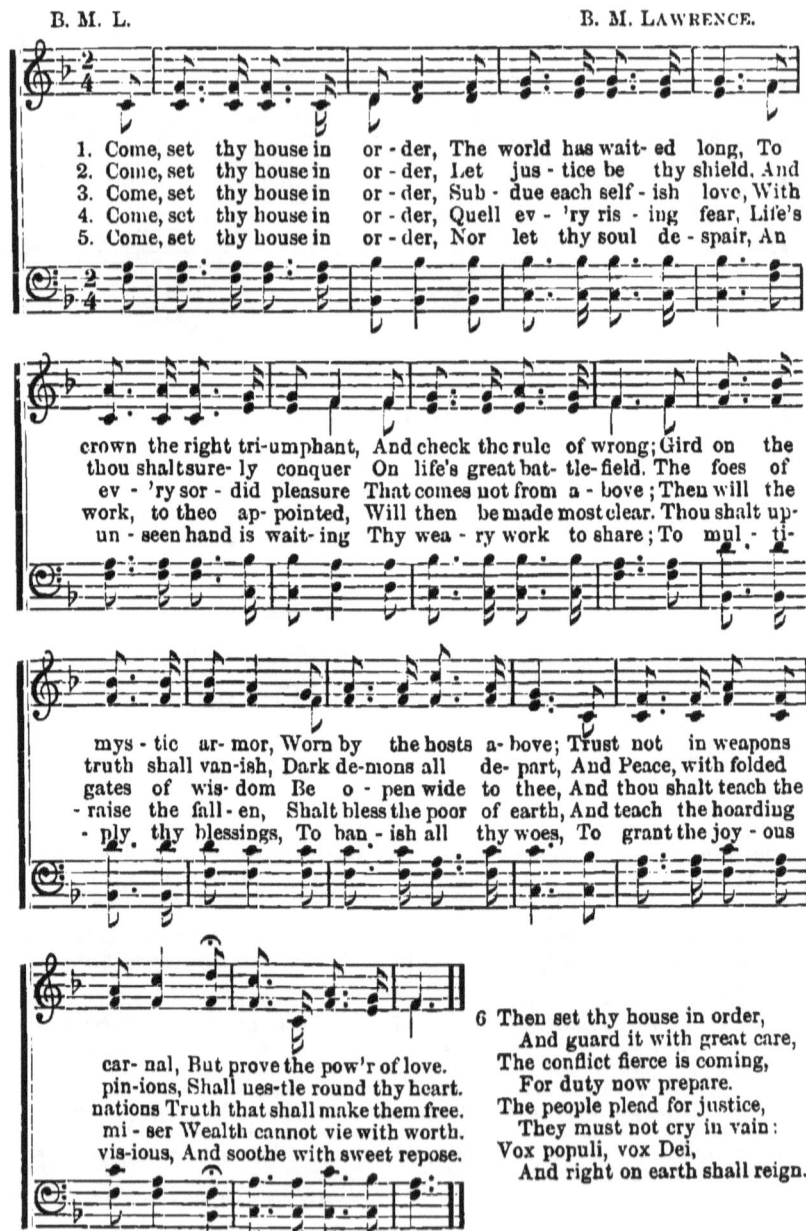

1. Come, set thy house in or-der, The world has wait-ed long, To crown the right tri-umphant, And check the rule of wrong; Gird on the mys-tic ar-mor, Worn by the hosts a-bove; Trust not in weapons car-nal, But prove the pow'r of love.
2. Come, set thy house in or-der, Let jus-tice be thy shield, And thou shalt sure-ly conquer On life's great bat-tle-field. The foes of truth shall van-ish, Dark de-mons all de-part, And Peace, with folded pin-ions, Shall nes-tle round thy heart.
3. Come, set thy house in or-der, Sub-due each self-ish love, With ev - 'ry sor - did pleasure That comes not from a - bove; Then will the gates of wis-dom Be o-pen wide to thee, And thou shalt teach the nations Truth that shall make them free.
4. Come, set thy house in or-der, Quell ev - 'ry ris - ing fear, Life's work, to thee ap-pointed, Will then be made most clear. Thou shalt up-raise the fall-en, Shalt bless the poor of earth, And teach the hoarding mi - ser Wealth cannot vie with worth.
5. Come, set thy house in or-der, Nor let thy soul de-spair, An un - seen hand is wait-ing Thy wea - ry work to share; To mul - ti-ply thy blessings, To ban - ish all thy woes, To grant the joy - ous vis-ious, And soothe with sweet repose.

6 Then set thy house in order,
And guard it with great care,
The conflict fierce is coming,
For duty now prepare.
The people plead for justice,
They must not cry in vain;
Vox populi, vox Dei,
And right on earth shall reign.

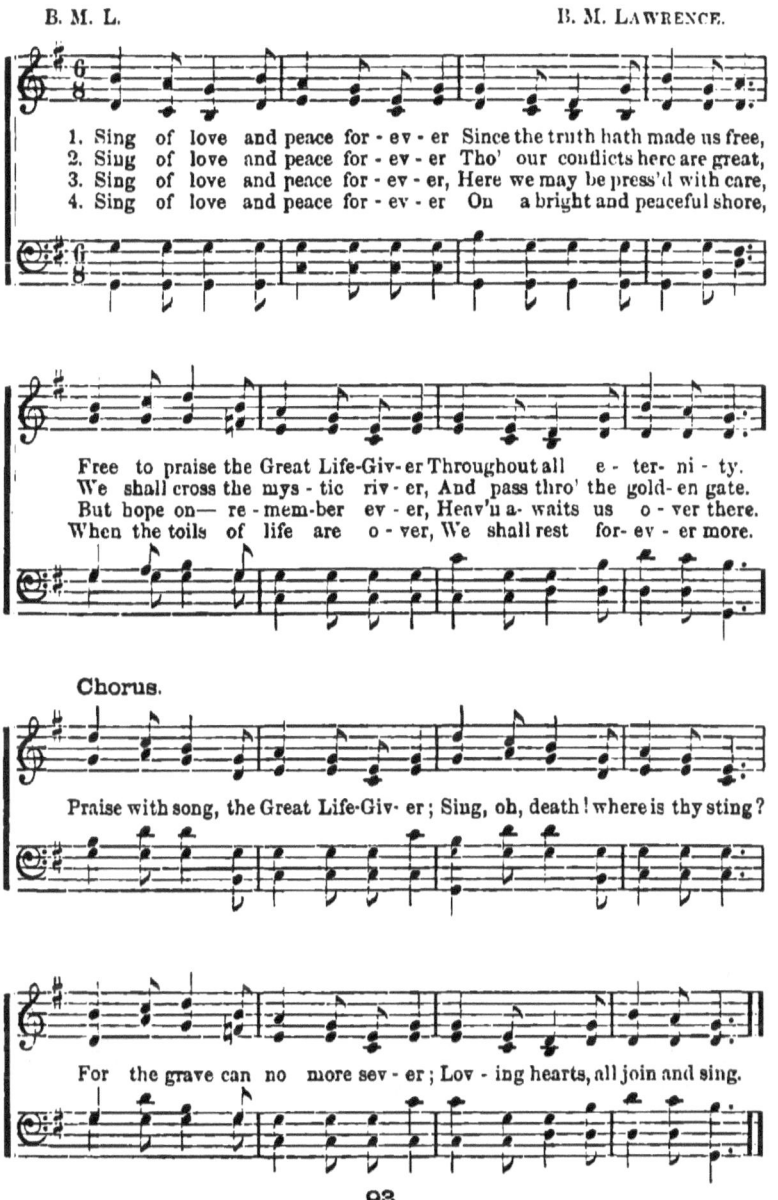

Oh, Think of that Home Over There.

"Neither can they die any more."—LUKE 20: 36.

B. M. L.
B. M. LAWRENCE.

1. Oh, think of that home o-ver there, Near the banks of the riv-er of peace, In this world there is naught to com-pare With the pleas-ures which there nev-er cease.
2. Oh, think of the peace o-ver there, Of dear loved ones who now are at rest, Far a-way from all sor-row and care, They are safe in that home of the blest.
3. Oh, think of the songs o-ver there, Sweet-est an-thems that nev-er seem old; Think of mu-sic that fills all the air, And of harps that are bright-er than gold.
4. Oh, think of that rest o-ver there, In the sweet land of love and de-light, End-less joys there at last we shall share, All ar-rayed in pure gar-ments of white.
5. Oh, think of our friends o-ver there, Who be-fore us have gone to that bourne, How they love to come back and de-clare: That the trav-'ler in-deed can re-turn.
6. Oh, think we shall live o-ver there, When the end of life's jour-ney has come; Then let each for that land now pre-pare, There all reap what they sow in that home.

Chorus.

O-ver there, o-ver there, o-ver there, Oh,

Oh, Think of that Home, Etc.—Concluded.

They Come to Thee.

"Who maketh His angels, spirits, His ministers."—PSA. 104: 4.

G. H. No. 51.   B. M. L.

1 They come to me, most cheerful thought,
With words of peace and rapture fraught,
A voice now whispers this to me:
"Thy angel-friends can come to thee."

CHORUS.—They come with love and sing with glee:
"And angel-hand now leadeth thee,
This truth indeed will make thee free,
An angel-hand now leadeth thee.

2 "Sometimes in paths of grief and gloom,
Again where sweetest flowers bloom,
Where e'er thou art, on land or sea,
An angel-hand still leadeth thee.—CHO.

3 "What joy to clasp their hands in thine,
To see their blissful faces shine;
They hear thy prayers and grant thy plea,
Sweet spirit-friends now come to thee.—CHO.

4 "When earth-life ends, when thy last breath
Shall triumph over pain and death,
The grave will gain no victory,
For angels then will come to thee."—CHO.

Beyond Life's Troubled Sea.

B. M. L.   B. M. LAWRENCE.

1. The man who casts the world a-side As little worth when once compared
2. Be-fore the light of woman's love; What sound so dear as her sweet voice?
3. Then, who would throw the wealth aside Of woman's love for earth's dull dross?

With woman's love, finds naught beside Such perfect bliss; he may have cared
No joys of earth or heav'n a-bove Can make the love-less heart re-joice.
She helps man stem life's swelling tide, And bears with him each bit-ter cross;

As mortals care for wealth and fame; For grandeur which makes glory bright,
True-mated souls care naught for show; The world's cold, hollow schemes they scorn;
Then, when thy yearning soul shall find An-oth-er heart all pure and free,

But hon-or is an emp-ty name, And glo-ry fades be-fore the light.
For lov-ing hearts can nev-er know The feel-ing of the word forlorn.
The twain let love's soft mesh-es bind As one be-yond life's troubled sea.

The Old Home of my Childhood.

B. M. L. B. M. LAWRENCE.

1. A-mong all the ten-der and hal-low-ed things That ev-er a-non sweet-est mem-o-ry brings, There is nothing more dear which the past now re-calls Than the old cottage home with its whitewashed walls.

2. How oft in the shade, a-down by the clear brook, For minnows we fished with a pin bent for hook, And with bare lit-tle feet how we loved to wade thro', And there each learned to paddle his own ca-noe.

3. That home made all welcome, this no one could doubt, The neighbors all knew that the latch-string was out, And there many the pil-grims that supp'd at its board, While the blazing log-fire in the fire-place roar'd.

Chorus.

How sweet is the thought which fond mem'ry recalls Of the old cottage home with its whitewashed walls.

4. Grand mansions to-day, although models of art,
Can never usurp its warm place in my heart;
Still the wild roses bloom in fond memory's halls
By the old cottage home with its whitewashed walls.

Walking Through the Valley.

To Miss M. W. M. on the loss of friends.

B. M. L.   B. M. LAWRENCE.

1. Thou art passing a-down the dark val-ley Where the shadows of death hedge thy way, But the storm-clouds of gloom, now so heav-y, Shall break forth in a bright gold-en day.
2. Tho' thy heart may feel sad and for-sak-en, And thy soul seem at times all cast down, Tho' thy trust in God's love may be sha-ken, Yet thy cross He will change to a crown.
3. With His rod and His staff He will sure-ly Bear thee on where heart aches are un-known, And when sor-rows shall gath-er a-round thee, He'll not leave thee to suf-fer a-lone.
4. And when dust un-to dust thou shalt min-gle, When the dear ones are lost from thy sight, Then let truth and love keep thine eye sin-gle, And by faith learn to walk in the light.

Chorus.

In the land where the rose blooms for-ev-er, Where they

Walking Through the Valley.—Concluded.

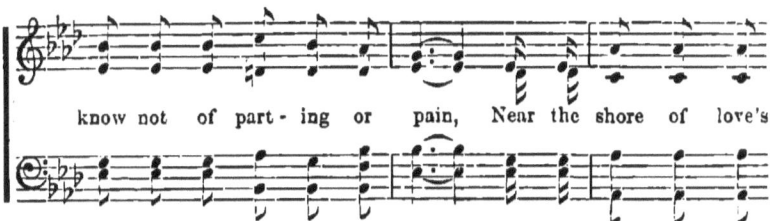

know not of part-ing or pain, Near the shore of love's

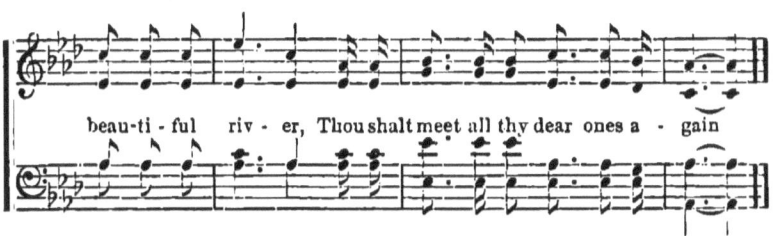

beau-ti-ful riv-er, Thou shalt meet all thy dear ones a-gain

In the Sweet Bye and Bye.

"Great is your reward in heaven."—MATT. 5: 12

G. H. No. 7. B. M L.

1.
When we meet beyond the river,
 In the sweet bye and bye,
We shall bless the Great Life-Giver
 In the sweet bye and bye;
There our deeds will all be known
When our life-work here is done,
We shall reap what we have sown
 In the sweet bye and bye.

2.
When we meet beyond the river,
 In the sweet bye and bye,
We shall part no more for ever
 In the sweet bye and bye;
There with rapture, oh, how sweet,
All our loved ones we shall greet,
Then our bliss will be complete
 In the sweet bye and bye

3.
When we meet beyond the river,
 In the sweet bye and bye,
Peace and joy will wed together,
 In the sweet bye and bye,
We shall all be known above
By our works of truth and love,
Good deeds will a passport prove
 In the sweet bye and bye.

4
When we meet beyond the river,
 In the sweet bye and bye,
Loving hearts no more shall sever
 In the sweet bye and bye;
There the grave will loose its gloom,
Sorrow no more shroud the tomb,
Flowers there will ever bloom
 In the sweet bye and bye.

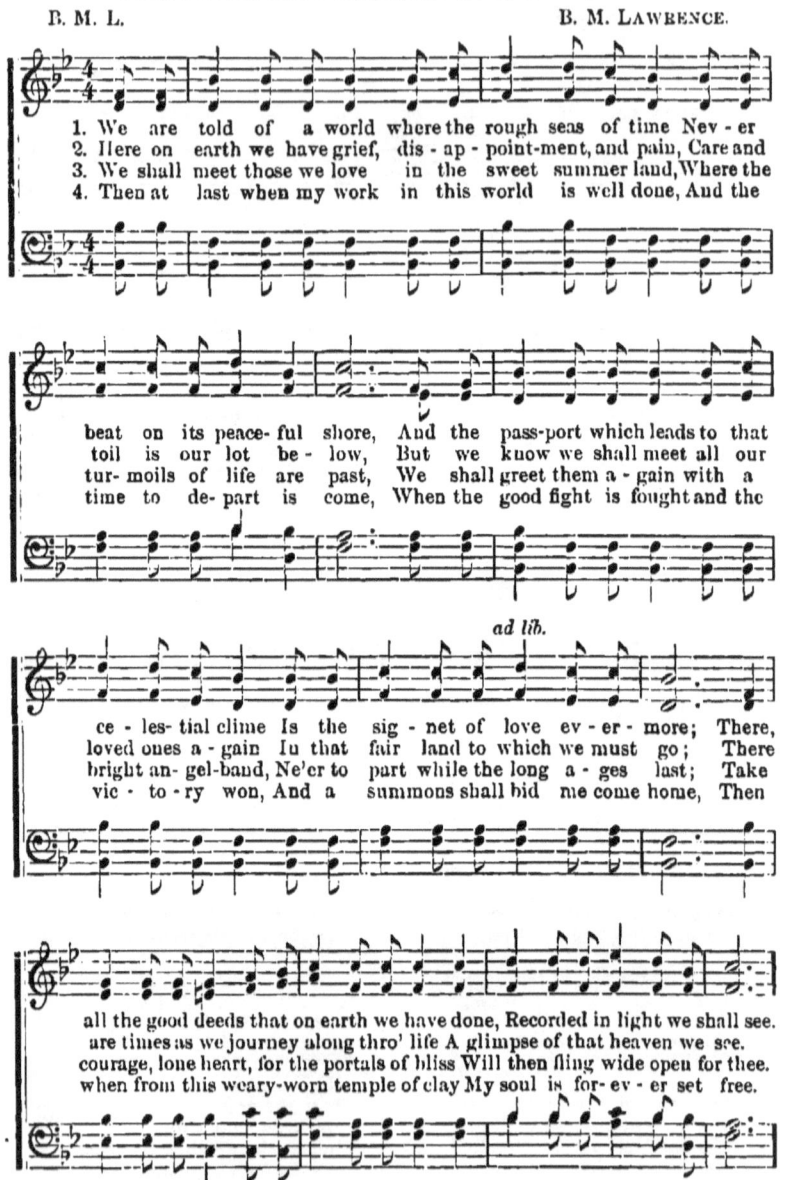

Waiting in Heaven for Me.—Concluded.

On the Evergreen Hills.—Concluded.

Remember the Brave Boys.—Concluded.

4 'Twas the fierce lust for gold wrought this ruin, Luke Rand,
   For it roused up the people to fight,
And it brought on defeat, both by sea and by land,
   To the brave men who fought with such might.
Mammon robs men of reason and love, Luke Rand,
   Makes a brother combat with his kin,
Turns a saint to a knave, makes the free man a slave,
   And is father to all forms of sin.

5 But a change in the land we have loved, Luke Rand,
   A change from the false to the true,
Brings to labor a hope that the time is at hand
   When the old shall give place to the new.
Then the right evermore shall prevail, Luke Rand,
   "Peace on earth" once again as of yore,
With a shout will ring forth, east and west, south and north,
   "Then the nations shall learn war no more."

The Mandate of Labor.

Air.—*The Star-Spangled Banner.*   B. M. L.

1 The Banner of Truth to the breeze is unfurled,
   And the Nations of earth against wrong are contending,
The Mandates of Labor have 'wakened the world,
   While the rights of all men her strong arm is defending.
      Her brave, gallant band
      Now make this demand:
That Robbers of Labor shall not rule the land.

        Chorus.

For the wealth made by toiling the Toilers must own,
And no man shall reap what another hath sown;
Yes, the wealth made by toiling the Toilers must own,
For no man should reap what his brother hath sown.

2 The people must learn that we all own the land,
   Then will they resolve these great wrongs shall be righted,
The right will succeed, for the time is at hand
   When the true friends of labor stand firmly united.
      Then thieves who by stealth
      Have secured boundless wealth,
Will all learn that labor is good for their health.—Cho.

3 Land, water, and air, which the whole nation owns,
   Are products of nature which God made free for all men,
And they must not be held by the great, idle drones,
   For the earth is the Lord's, made for all of His children.
      Brave men, true as steel,
      Must make robbers feel
The force of God's law which says, "Thou shalt not steal."—Cho.

4 The battle has come and oppression must fall,
   By soldiers of peace bearing banners of Labor,
"With malice toward none," but with justice to all,
   Comes the reign of "good-will" to man and his neighbor.
      For truth cannot fail;
      The right will prevail,
And the demon of fraud is beginning to quail.—Cho.

The Noble Workingman. Concluded.

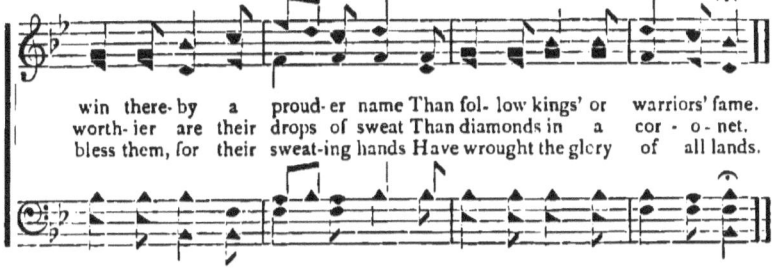

win there-by a proud-er name Than fol-low kings' or warriors' fame.
worth-ier are their drops of sweat Than diamonds in a cor - o - net.
bless them, for their sweat-ing hands Have wrought the glcry of all lands.

Abou Ben Adhem.

LEIGH HUNT.   B. M. LAWRENCE.

Abou Ben Adhem, may his tribe increase! Awoke one night from a deep dream of peace, And | saw within the moonlight of his room, | Making it light, and like the lily in bloom, ||
An | angel, writing in a | book of | gold. ||
Exceeding peace had made Ben Adhem bold, And to the presence in his room, he said: What | writest | thou? " ||
The vision raised its head, And with a look, made | all of sweet ac- | cord, ||
Answered, "The names of those that | love the | Lord. ||
"And is mine one?" said Abou. | "Nay, not so," Replied the angel. | Abou spoke more low, But cheerily ||
Still, and | said, | "I pray thee, then, Write me as one that ||
Loves his fellow | men." ||
The angel wrote and vanished. The next night He came again with great awakening light, | And showed the names whom love of | God had | blest, ||
When | lo! Ben Adhem's name led | all the | rest. ||

The World Will be the Better for it.

B. M. L.   B. M. Lawrence.

1. When man shall keep the great command, Feel-ing the same for self and neighbor; When right shall rule in ev-'ry land; When all shall live by hon-est la-bor; When jus-tice, love, and pur-i-ty Bring peace on earth with nought to mar it; When all shall be By truth made free, The world will be the bet-ter for it.

2. When men care less for crowns of gold, Lay-ing up treas-ure more by giv-ing To feed and clothe the poor and cold, And teach them bet-ter ways of liv-ing; When men of wealth are more in-clined To buy the truth—love and a-dore it; When all man-kind Prize worth of mind, The world will be the bet-ter for it.

The World Will be, Etc.—Concluded.

3.

When men care less for what folks say,
   And take more care to curb their passions;
When women shall refuse to pay
   Allegiance unto useless fashions;
When she shall never more compress
   Her form divine, nor dare to mar it;
     When all care less
     For show and dress,
   The world will be the better for it.

4.

When men care less for gin and rum,
   And less for wine, ale, beer and brandy,
For nostrums which the nerves benumb,
   For poison drugs or pills of candy;
When men shall eat the purest food,
   Refuse tobacco and abhor it;
     When reason's ken
     Shall govern men,
   The world will be the better for it

5.

When men care less for forms and creeds,
   And more for apostolic preaching;
When men serve Christ by noble deeds,
   And hearken to the Spirit's teaching;
When men will not deny the truth,
   Nor by wrong-doing pierce and scar it;
     When all shall know
     A heaven below,
   The world will be the better for it.

6.

When paradise on earth is found,
   And converse held with seraph wardens;
When Eden homes for all abound,
   Where pure love dwells in peaceful gardens;
When all may own and dress the earth,
   Till golden grain and fruits bend o'er it;
     From want secure;
     None rich—none poor,
   The world will be the better for it.

The World Would be the Better for it.

1.

If men cared less for wealth and fame,
   And less for battle-fields and glory;
If writ in human hearts a name
   Seemed better than in song or story;
If men, instead of nursing pride,
   Would learn to hate it and abhor it;
     If more relied
     On love to guide,
   The world would be the better for it.

2.

If men dealt less in stocks and lands,
   And more in bonds and deeds fraternal;
If love's work had more willing hands
   To link this world to the supernal;
If men stored up love's oil and wine,
   And on bruised human hearts would pour it;
     If yours and mine
     Would once combine,
   The world would be the better for it.

3.

If more would act the play of life,
   And fewer spoil it in rehersal;
If bigotry would sheath its knife,
   Till good became more universal;
If custom, gay with ages grown,
   Had fewer blind men to adore it;
     If talent shone
     In Truth alone,
   The world would be the better for it.

4.

If men were wise in little things,
   Affecting less in all their dealings;
If hearts had fewer rusted strings
   To isolate their kindly feelings;
If men, when Wrong beats down the Right,
   Would strike together and restore it;
     If right made might
     In every fight,
   The world would be the better for it.

The Rum Maker's Remorse.

"Woe unto the men of strength who mingle strong drink."—ISA. 5: 22.

B. M. L. B. M. LAWRENCE.

1. If the past we could nev-er re-call, Bar-tien, Which has fled with our hopes long a-go, If its dark deeds and mem-o-ries all, Bartien, Would sleep while we lin-ger be-low; Were the fount-ains of ru-in all dry, Bar-tien, And
2. When we think of the beer we have brewed, Bar-tien, From the bins filled with bright golden grain, While the hun-gry were cry-ing for food, Bartien, And beg-ging for shel-ter in vain; When we think of the ill-got-ten gold, Bar-tien, Which
3. When we look to the lone pot-ter's field, Bar-tien, Where the chil-dren of pov-er-ty sleep, There the ru-in of rum is re-vealed, Bartien, Till the an-gels in heav'n must weep; 'Twas the root of all e-vil we own, Bar-tien, Drove sweet

114

The Rum Maker's Remorse.—Concluded.

hushed ev - 'ry gin mak- ing mill,   If the wrongs we have done
came to our cof - fers for rum,   Then a thought of the starv -
peace from our path far a - way,   And while rea - son re- mains

could but die,   Bartien, We might hope for some hap- pi-ness still.
- ing and cold,   Bartien, Brings re - grets that we can - not o'er-come.
on its throne,   Bartien, We must ev - er re - gret the dark day.

Chorus.

But re- morse ev- er broods o'er the grave,   Bartien, Of hopes which our
While re- morse ev- er broods o'er the grave,   Bartien, Of hopes which our
For re- morse ev- er broods o'er the grave,   Bartien, Of hopes which our

hearts no more fill,   And the deep sea of sor - row's dark

wave, Bar - tien, Rolls in bil - lows that peace can - not still.

Who Hath Woe?

"Woe unto them that follow strong drink."—ISA. 5: 11.

B. M. L.   F. L. ARMSTRONG.

1 Woe unto them that rise up early | in the | morning, ||
   That they may follow after strong fer- | mented | wine; ||
   Who disregard the inspired prophet's | faithful | warning, ||
   And prostitute the wholesome product | of the | vine; |

2 Who mar the music of the social | feast by | drinking ||
   That which defiles the body and de- | stroys the | brain; ||
   Which captivates and kills the noblest | powers of | thinking, ||
   Enthroning selfish lusts with beastly | greed of | grain. ||

3 Woe to the mighty multitude, dried | up with | thirsting, ||
   Hungering for that which fails to nourish | and sus- | tain ;
   Which call for more while maddened brain with | wine is | bursting, ||
   And nature's still small voice calls out for | help in | vain. ||

4 Shame on the men of honor! legal | men of | learning, ||
   False teachers who, for lack of knowledge, | lead a- | stray ||
   The toiling masses who are wildly | pleading, | yearning |
   For light to guide their weary feet in | wisdom's | way. |

5 Woe unto them that call good evil, | who de- | filing ||
   God's dwelling-place, the temple made for | His a- | bode; ||
   Who break the law, pervert the sense, the | taste be- | guiling ||
   With bitter things which all the baser | feelings | goad. ||

6 Woe to the mighty men of strength, who | strong drink | mingle, ||
   Inflamed by wine, they live to grati- | fy their | lust; ||
   Devoid of love, like sounding brass or | tinkling | cymbal, ||
   Their root shall die, their blossom shall go | up as | dust. ||

7 Therefore, as the burning fire shall de- | stroy the | stubble, ||
   And as the flame consumeth chaff be- | fore the | wind, ||
   So shall wine drinkers find reward in | woe and | trouble, ||
   But temperance and purity brings | peace of | mind. ||

8 Their sons shall walk and not be weary, | shall not | stumble, ||
   Nor shall they slumber as the stupid | drunkards' | sleep; ||
   They shall be fed with bounty, filled with | spirits | humble; ||
   "With love for all" malice for none, God's | laws they | keep. ||

Peace on Earth Once More.

No. 1. Tune—G. H., No. 14.

"And there shall be no more death."—*Rev.* xxi. 4.

1 Earth and Heaven now are blending,
  Light at last appears,
  Angels from above descending,
  Come to quell our fears.

CHORUS.

Hail the truth, a light is shining
From the other shore,
While the loved ones are returning
Back to earth once more.

2 They have come, the grave defeating,
  Making death our friend,
  And they sing these words, repeating,
  "Life will never end."   *Cho.*

3 Truth will triumph, right ordains it,
  And the time draws nigh;
  Peace and progress both proclaim it,
  "Souls can never die."   *Cho.*

4 Earth, long years in sorrow wailing,
  Finds relief from woe,
  Deeds of love to man prevailing,
  Will bring Heav'n below.   *Cho.*

5 Hark, the hosts on high are singing,
  "Good will to all men,
  Souls still live"—the chorus ringing,
  "Peace on earth shall reign."   *Cho.*
                                  B. M. L.

The Soul's Sweet Home.

No. 2. Tune—G. H., No. 84, Vol. III.

"Ye shall see heaven op'n, and the angels."—*John* i. 51.

1 There is a land of fruits and vines,
  Of golden grains and living wines,
  Where night and death have passed away,
  And life is one long blissful day.

CHORUS.

Sweet summer land, sweet summer land,
Sometimes in dreams I seem to stand,
And look beyond life's stormy sea,
Where mansions bright are made for me,
And view with joy the shining shore,
The soul's sweet home forevermore.

2 Bright angels come and greet us here;
  With them we hold communion dear,
  They come and clasp us by the hand,
  And point us to that better land.

3 Ofttimes they come with words of love,
  And tell us of their home above;
  Again they bring a sweet perfume,
  With brightest flowers in full bloom.

4 They chant sweet music over there,
  The songs of love float on the air,
  Where jarring discords never come,
  There we shall find the soul's sweet home.
                                  B. M. L.

That Valley of Peace.

No. 3. Tune—G. H., No. 62, Vol. III.

"And there shall be no night there."—*Rev.* xxii. 5.

1 We sing of that valley of peace,
  With rivers of pleasure so rare,
  Where sunlight and love never cease;—
  Oh, what must it be to be there!

CHORUS.

To be there, to be there,
The joys of the angels to share;
To be there, to be there,
Oh, what must it be to be there!

2 We sing of the mansions above,
  The robes of pure white we shall wear,
  The music and harps made of love;—
  Oh, what must it be to be there!

3 We sing of our friends in that home
  Beyond earthly sorrow and care,
  And think of the sweet joys to come;—
  Oh, what must it be to be there!

4 We sing of that soul-world sublime,
  With skies ever cloudless and fair;
  We dream of that beautiful clime;—
  Oh, what must it be to be there!

5 We sing of that immortal shore,
  With which there is nought to compare,
  There loved ones will part nevermore;—
  Oh, what must it be to be there!
                                  B. M. L.

Where Flowers Ever Bloom.

No. 4. Tune—G. H., No. 40, Vol. III.

"A new heaven and a new earth."—*Rev.* xxi. 1.

1 We have heard of a world far away,
  Where they know not of sorrow or care;
  Where the sunlight of love makes it day,
  And they have no more night over there.

CHORUS.

Over there, over there, over there,
We shall meet on that ever-green shore;
Over there, over there, over there, [more.
We shall meet there to part never-

2 We have heard that our friends who pass on
  Are asleep in the dark silent tomb;
  But we know that they only have gone
  To that land where the flow'rs ever
                          bloom.   *Cho.*

3 We have heard when they go to that
                          bourne,
  They remain there in torment or bliss;
  But the trav'ler we know can return,
  For they come back from that land to
                          this.   *Cho.*

4 Oh, we know there is peace, joy and rest,
  And a home for the pilgrim above;
  Yet to gain that bright land of the blest,
  We must purchase our passport with
  love.   *Cho.*   B. M. L.

The Gates Ajar For All.

No. 5. Tune—G. H., No. 15.

"The gates of it shall not be shut."—*Rev.* xxi. 25.

1 The gates of glory stand ajar,
  And through the portals gleaming
  Sweet angel friends come from afar,
  With love their faces beaming.

CHORUS.
The pearly gates, what joy to see,
Are left ajar for you and me,
  For you and me,
For all by truth made free.

2 The gates are open wide for all,
  From every tribe and nation,
  For rich or poor, for great or small,
  From every rank and station. *Cho.*

3 Proclaim the truth and gain a crown,
  This gospel must be spoken, [frown,
  Press onward, then, though foes may
  And win love's royal token. *Cho.*

4 Beyond the river's brink once more,
  Friends that to death were given
  Will meet us on the other shore,
  And love us still in heaven. *Cho.*

5 The gates of glory, oh, how grand!
  Across the mystic river,
  They open to the summer land,
  Where we shall live forever. *Cho.*
  B. M. L.

Death to Alcohol.

No. 6. Tune—G. H., No. 14.

"Wine is a mocker."—*Prov.* xx. 1.

1 Friends of temp'rance, take fresh courage,
  Right will gain the day;
  True reform is now the watchword,
  Wisdom leads the way.

CHORUS.
Join the ranks, uphold the banner,
  Old King Rum must fall,
Join the ranks and give no quarter;
  Death to Alcohol!

2 Now the temp'rance host is marching,
  Wrong must surely fail;
  Long or short though fierce the conflict,
  Right will yet prevail. *Cho.*

3 Brave young men are daily falling—
  See this deadly foe,
  Filling all the land with mourning,
  Hear the wail of woe! *Cho.*

4 When the temp'rance cause shall triumph,
  Woman can proclaim
  To the captives of the wine cup,
  Freedom in Christ's name. *Cho.*

5 Onward, then, ye hosts of true men;
  Cheer, brave comrades, cheer;
  By the help of God and woman,
  Victory is near. *Cho.* B. M. L.

Lead Us in the Light.

No. 7. Tune—G. H., No. 99, Vol. II.

"They shall bear thee up."—*Ps.* xci. 12.

1 Come, angels, lead us in the light,
  Come, prove that life can never cease,
  With wisdom guide our ways aright,
  And lead our feet in paths of peace.

CHORUS.
Come, angels, come, and guide our feet
  In paths of peace to that bright shore
Beyond the tide; there may we meet
  With those we love, to part no more.

2 Lift up our thoughts from earthly care,
  Away to that bright world above,
  And make us feel that over there
  Rewards will come for works of love.

3 Though oft mid daily scenes of life,
  With toil and care we must contend,
  Secure us from turmoil and strife,
  And prove to each a constant friend.

4 Help us to share our brother's grief,
  The goodness in his heart to see,
  Sad, gloomy souls to give relief,
  And make men peaceful, pure and free.

5 When from this earth we pass away,
  To live with loved ones gone before,
  Then may we hear the angels say,
  Sweet peace is thine forevermore.
  B. M. L.

We Shall Meet By and By.

No. 8. Tune—G. H., No. 85.

"Wherefore comfort yourselves together."—
I Thess. v. 11.

1 Wondrous truth, what joy to know
  Souls who leave this world below,
  When they reach the other shore,
  Can return to earth once more.

CHORUS.
We shall meet them by and by,
  Meet them on that peaceful shore,
We shall meet them by and by,
  Meet them there, to part no more.

2 We shall meet them over there,
  Far beyond this world of care;
  In that blissful home above,
  We shall meet all those we love. *Cho.*

3 We shall know and there be known,
  Where all reap what they have sown,
  And when earth's work is well done,
  Life will seem but just begun. *Cho.*

4 We shall mingle with the blest,
  In that land of peace and rest,
  Gaining still a strength of soul,
  While the ceaseless ages roll. *Cho.*

5 We shall chant songs new and old,
  And our lives will still unfold,
  On that bright, immortal shore,
  Upward still forevermore. *Cho.*
  B. M. L.

Safe at Home, from Sorrow Free.
No. 9. Tune—G. H., No. 87, Vol. III.

"*In my Father's house.*"—*John* xiv. 2.

1 There, safe at home, from all sorrow set
    free,
  When we join the blest angels above,
What a blissful band of saints we shall see,
  In that sweet land of sunshine and love.
Disease and woe, disappointment and
    pain,
  Will come in that pure world no more,
For grief and care, with dark clouds of
    despair,
  Are unknown on that beautiful shore

CHORUS.
Safe, safe at home, our own sweet, sweet
  Forever on that shore,   [home,
We'll sing of love in that home above,
  Where grief and care shall come no more

2 There safe at home, in that pure land of
    light,   [run;
  We shall rest when our race here is
There to meet with loved ones enrobed
    in white,
  Will be heaven indeed begun;
Chanting sweet notes, which the choris-
    ters swell,
  With anthems that never seem old,
Songs of pure love will re-echo above,
  With a rapture that cannot be told.
                               B. M. L.

Touch Not, Taste Not, Handle Not.
No. 10. Tune—G. H., No. 35, Vol. III.

"*Which all are to perish.*"—*Col.* ii. 22.

1 Then touch not thou the unclean thing,
  Preserve thy temple undefiled,
Make it the home—fit dwelling place
  For a chaste spirit—meek and mild.
No longer be the slave of vice;
  Henceforth be free—break every bond;
Let not base loves and sordid aims
  Dwarf and deform thy soul beyond.

2 Then taste not thou the unclean thing,
  It will but lure thy soul to death,
Defile the body, cloud the mind,
  Polluting both thy thoughts and breath.
Inhale pure air, not poison fumes,
  Reject whatever leads to crime,
To idle thoughts, foul words and deeds,
  Which stain the soul throughout all
    time.

3 Then handle not the unclean thing;
  This law divine was made for all;
"Obey the perfect rules of health."
  Nature proclaims as well as Paul:
"The filthy shall be filthy still,"
  For death does not transform the soul,
Then break the yoke, throw off the spell,
  Ere appetite gains full control. B. M. L.

Beyond the Beautiful River.
No. 11. Tune—Key of Eb.

"*A pure river of water of life.*"—*Rev.* xxii. 1.

1 We shall meet beyond the river,
  In our glorious home above,
There with dearest friends forever
  Live in perfect peace and love.

CHORUS.
We shall meet beyond the river,
  The beautiful, the beautiful river;
Gather with our friends at the river
  Which flows by the soul's sweet home.

2 On the bright shores of the river,
  With its silver-gleaming spray,
Gems of beauty we shall gather,
  Through the endless June-clad day.

3 Close beside the shining river,
  With dear loved ones we shall roam,
When we meet no more to sever
  In the soul's sweet summer home.

4 When we reach the peaceful river
  We shall lay our burdens down,
There with true souls we shall ever
  Wear a white robe and a crown.

5 When at last we cross the river,
  All our anxious cares will cease,
While we bless the Great Life-Giver
  Through the endless years of peace.
                               B. M. L

Angels Whisper They Can Come.
No. 12. Tune—G. H., No 69.

"*Thy dead shall live awake and sing.*"--*Is.* xxvi.19.

1 They can come—oh, blessed thought—
  Words with so much rapture fraught.
Now the veil is rent between
  This world and the world unseen.
From the bright supernal home
  Angels whisper, "They can come."

2 They can come—souls that we love—
  From their peaceful homes above;
And their words of hope and cheer
  Fall in rapture on my ear.
For the regal guests make room;
  Bid them welcome—they can come.

3 They can come when sorrows press,
  Come and make our trials less;
Come and banish doubts and fears,
  Swell our joys and dry our tears,
Conquer death, and, from the tomb,
  Take all terror—they can come.

4 They can come—they are not dead;
  Let the feast of love be spread.
They have only gone before
  To the blest, immortal shore.
Mansions there for us have room,
  With the angels. They can come.
                               B. M. L.

We Know it Must be True.

No. 13. Tune—G. H., No. 53.

"Work out your own salvation."—*Phil.* ii. 12.

1 Must we place on the lowly,
  The well-beloved Son,
  Whose life was pure and holy,
  The wrong deeds we have done?

CHORUS.

Then "work out your own salvation
  With fear and trembling," too;
Says the voice of inspiration,
  We know it must be true.

2 Whoso the wrong act doeth
  Should suffer for the deed;
Thus saith the law and gospel,
  And thus should say the creed. *Cho.*

3 Each for himself must suffer,
  For every crime atone;
And here, or else hereafter,
  All reap what they have sown. *Cho.*

4 The heathen have their scapegoats,
  With sins away they flee;
But will God punish goodness,
  And leave the guilty free? *Cho.*

5 To lay our sins on Jesus,
  And make him bear the blame,
Would surely be injustice,
  An outrage and a shame. *Cho.*

6 Nothing but truth will free us,
  From guilt and sin we know;
For endless peace prepare us,
  And wash us white as snow. *Cho.*

B. M. L.

The Golden Age Draws Nigh.

No. 14. Tune—G. H., No. 110.

"They sung as it were a new song before the throne."—*Rev.* xiv. 3.

1 Joy to the world, for Light is come;
  Again bright angels bring
Good will to souls in every home,
  Then let all nations sing.

2 Joy to the world, for Wisdom reigns,
  Let men her ways approve;
While seraphs, with celestial strains,
  Repeat our songs of love.

3 Joy to the world, for Truth appears
  To make all nations free;
While angels, from the highest spheres,
  Proclaim earth's jubilee.

4 Joy to the world, for Love is king,
  Endowed with power and grace,
Let peace and progress join and sing:
  He reigns with righteousness.

5 Joy to the world and heaven above,
  Old dogmas now must die;
Right comes to rule men's lives with love;
  The golden age draws nigh. B. M. L.

There to Part no More.

No. 15. Tune—G. H., No. 38, Vol. III.

"Which hope we have as an anchor."—*Heb.* vi. 19.

1 When all the chords of earth-life shall sever,
  And the boatman pale shall come,
Then we shall cross o'er the lone dark river,
  There to meet with friends at home.

CHORUS.

Safe over there will the dear ones greet us,
  On that bright eternal shore,
With joyful songs they will come to meet us,
  Meet us, meet us there to part no more.

2 When we have gained that bright world of flowers,
  Where the fruits immortal grow,
There, 'mid the peaceful, love-blooming bowers,
  We shall find release from woe.

3 With perfect love and good-will to neighbor,
  When at last our course is run,
Then we shall look back on life's past labor,
  And a voice will say, "Well done!"

4 Friends that we love over there will greet us,
  All arrayed in robes of white, [us,
With joyful songs will the angels meet
  Meet us in that land of light.

B. M. L.

Going Home To-morrow.

No. 16. Tune—G. H., No. 22.

"A house eternal in the heavens."—*2 Cor.* 5. 1.

1 We're going home where angels roam,
  Beyond the reach of sorrow,
Where none shall wear the brow of care,
  We're going home to-morrow.

CHORUS.

We're going home away from care and sorrow,
We're going home, we're going home to-morrow.

2 Here weary feet oft press the street,
  There all is bright and golden,
Here hearts will ache, there angels wake
  Long-lost loves sweet and olden. *Cho.*

3 Then do not weep for those who sleep
  Within the grave so narrow,
Beyond the skies their spirits rise,—
  We're going home to-morrow. *Cho.*

4 With endless joy without alloy,
  Where death no more shall sever,
There we shall see our friends and be
  At home with them forever. *Cho.*

B. M. L.

The Voice of Truth.

No. 17. Tune—G. H , No. 35.

"Whatsoever a man soweth, that shall he also reap."—*Eph.* v. 7.

1 The voice of Truth doth say,
　"However great or small,
　Each his own debts must pay—
　　One should not pay for all."

　　　CHORUS.
　The voice of Truth revere:
　"Pay all the debts you owe;
This will make thy conscience clear,
　And wash thee white as snow."

2 His burden each should bear,
　Not load down one alone;
So great a wrong would sear
　A heart as hard as stone. *Cho.*

3 All men still love the right,
　And none are free from blame;
Can blood wash dark souls white,
　While sin remains the same? *Cho.*

4 When from a dying bed
　Thy spirit shall arise,
Each debt must then be paid,
　For justice never dies. *Cho.*

5 Before a righteous Lord
　The soul will then be brought,
To answer for each word,
　For every deed and thought. *Cho.*

6 Reward will then be given
　For all that thou hast done;
There at the court of heaven
　All reap what they have sown. *Cho.*
　　　　　　　　　　　　　B. M. L.

The Pilgrim Going Home.

No. 18. Tune—G. H., No. 49, Vol. II.

"Shall inherit all things."—*Rev.* xxi. 7.

1 Pilgrims of progress here,
　While going home;
Ofttimes our way is drear, etc.;
Strife, care and sorrow stand
　Round us on every hand,
But in the Summer Land,
　There is our home.

2 What though our feet grow sore,
　While going home,
Joys we shall find in store, etc.;
Clouds may our skies o'ercast,
Rudely may blow the blast,
Yet when the storm is past,
　We shall go home.

3 Sweet spirit friends we know,
　While going home,
Come to us here below, etc.;
Among the pure and blest,
With those we love the best,
We all at last shall rest,
　Safe, safe at home. B. M. L.

Hear the Voice of Truth.

No. 19. Tune—G. H., No. 40, Vol. II.

"The truth shall make you free."—*John* viii. 32.

1 The voice of truth supreme
　Proclaims through all the land,
That wrong must vanish like a dream,
　But right shall ever stand.

　　　CHORUS.
Hear the still, small voice
　Calling unto thee:
Choose the truth; take wisdom's choice;
　The truth will make thee free.

2 The voice of truth speaks clear
　To every list'ning heart,
If men would only pause to hear,
　Wise lore it will impart. *Cho.*

3 The voice of truth has power
　To crumble thrones to dust;
Before it kings and pontiffs cower,
　The sword and scepter rust. *Cho.*

4 The voice of truth confirms
　What seers of old have seen,
And tells us now in plainer terms
　What ancient scriptures mean. *Cho.*

5 The voice of truth and love
　Would lead away from vice,
And make this world, like heaven above,
　A peaceful paradise. *Cho.*

6 Then hail the voice of truth;
　All hail from shore to shore.
More dear than everlasting youth;
　All hail, forevermore! *Cho.* B. M. L.

Heaven is Our Home.

No. 20. Tune—G. H., No. 49, Vol. II.

"An house not made with hands."—*II Cor.* v. 1.

1 When all our work is done,
　Heaven is our home;
When life's short race is run,
　Heaven is our home.
Here we have trials sore,
But on a brighter shore,
Where pain shall come no more—
　Heaven is our home.

2 Here sorrow clouds our way—
　Heaven is our home;
Where there is endless day—
　Heaven is our home.
There all is peace and love,
In that blest world above,
Where friends all faithful prove,
　Heaven is our home.

3 Beyond the reach of care—
　Heaven is our home;
Dear friends await us there—
　Heaven is our home.
Then welcome to the tomb,
Farewell to want and gloom,
Where flowers ever bloom—
　Heaven is our home. B. M. L.

Lay Up Treasure In Heaven.

No. 21. Tune—G. H., No. 11.

"Lay not up treasures on earth."—*Matt.* vi. 19.

1 Wayfaring pilgrims on earth among
 strangers, [pursue;
 The long, weary journey of life we
 Our pathway is daily surmounted with
  dangers, [view.
 Then let us forever keep heaven in

CHORUS.
 Oh, there lay up treasures,
 Oh, there lay up treasures,
 Where love, peace and pleasure
 Will reign evermore.

2 Each day with kind deeds of love lay up
  treasures
 Above, where bold robbers break not
  through and steal, [measure
 And mete to thy brother exactly the
 We wish him to give us when with
  him we deal. *Cho.*

3 Seek out the poor, who are weighed
  down with sadness, [disgrace;
 Stark poverty ofttimes is free from
 The joy will rebound which brings thy
  brother gladness,
 Then think what would please thee
  wert thou in his place. *Cho.*

4 Eyes that we see not forever are keeping
 A record in heaven of all deeds that
  we do; [long be reaping,
 Each seed sown on earth we shall ere
 Then we shall rejoice if our lives have
  been true. *Cho.*
 B. M. L.

The Light of That Land is Love.

No. 22. Tune—G. H., No. 22, Vol. III.

"Eye hath not seen, nor ear heard."—*I Cor.* ii. 9.

1 Eye hath not seen, ear hath not heard,
 Of the bliss in store above,
 No mortal can speak the wonderful word,
 For the light of that land is love.

CHORUS.
 There is no more night in that world of
  That glorious home above, [light,
 There all join and sing, till the echoes ring,
 "Oh, the light of that land is love."

2 We have heard from lips of humble seers,
 And their words our hearts approve,
 That loved ones who come from those
  bright spheres,
 Say "the light of that world is love."

3 Sometimes while in dreams our souls will
  flee,
 As on wings of homing dove,
 That peaceful rest then we seem to see,
 And the light of that land is love.
 B. M. L.

Sweet Home of the Soul.

No. 23. Tune—G. H., No. 20.

"I will sing with the spirit."—*I Cor.*, xiv. 15.

1 I will sing the glad song
  Of that ever green shore,
 That sweet summer home of the soul,
  Where the storms never beat
  Nor the dark billows roar,
 While the years of eternity roll,
 While the years of eternity roll ;
  Where the storms never beat
  Nor the dark billows roar,
 While the years of eternity roll.

2 In that home of the soul,
  While in visions and dreams,
 No tongue can describe what I see,
  And at times there is only
  A thin veil, it seems,
 Between that fair country and me,
 Between that fair country and me ;
  And at times, etc.

3 Oh, that beautiful home
  Is for you and for me,
 For all have dear friends on that shore ;
  When life's work is done,
  And the soul shall go home,
 We'll meet them to part nevermore,
 We'll meet them to part nevermore ;
  When life's work, etc.

4 Oh, how blest we shall be
  In that glorious land,
 When free from all sorrow and pain,
  There with harps and white robes
  We shall join the bright band,
 And meet all our loved ones again,
 And meet all our loved ones again ;
  There with harps, etc. B. M. L.

Nearer, My God, To Thee.

No. 24. Tune—G. H., No. 118.

"Draw near to God."—*Ps.* lxxiii. 28.

1 Nearer, my God, to thee;
  Nearer to thee;
 E'en though it be a cross
  That raiseth me,
 Still all my song shall be, etc.

2 Though like the wanderer,
  The sun gone down,
 Darkness be over me,
  My rest a stone,
 Yet in my dreams I'd be, etc.

3 There let the way appear
  Steps unto heaven ;
 All that thou sendest me
  In mercy given;
 Angels to beckon me, etc.

4 Then with my waking thoughts,
  Bright with thy praise,
 Out of my stony griefs,
  Bethel I'll raise ;
 So by my woes to be, etc.

The Pilgrim's Plea for Prayer.
No. 25. Tune—G. H., No. 29

"The prayer of the righteous man."—*Jas.* v. 16.

1 Pilgrims on life's thorny pathway,
 Needless burdens we must bear,
When by faith we fail to carry
 All our wants to heaven in prayer.
Life is full of sore temptations,
 Trials meet us everywhere,
But we ever must remember
 We can find relief in prayer.

2 Angel friends are ever near us,
 All our joys and griefs to share,
And they never fail to hear us
 When our hearts pour out in prayer.
They are always true and faithful,
 Guarding us with tender care,
And they long to heal our heartaches,
 When we go to them in prayer.

3 When the soul is sorrow-laden,
 Overcome with grief and care,
Unseen hands will bring us comfort,
 If we plead for help in prayer.
Sho ld all earthly friends forsake thee,
 Seek for solace over there,
Loving angel arms will shield thee,
 Only look to them in prayer.

4 When the voyage of life is ended,
 Then, in mansions bright and fair,
We shall meet the blessed angels
 Who have heard and answered prayer.
Then with songs of peace and gladness,
 All arrayed in vestments rare,
We shall sing celestial sonnets,
 Praising Him who hears all prayer.
 B. M. L.

The Sands of Time are Flowing.
No. 26. Tune—G. H., No. 61, Vol. II.

"To be absent from the body."—*II Cor.*v. 8.

1 The sands of time are flowing fast,
 The race will soon be run,
Our work on earth will then be past,
 And rest in heaven begun.

CHORUS.
Then come, angels, come,
 Oh, come and take us home,
Come, bear us away on your wings of love,
 To that immortal shore,
To meet once again with dear ones above,
 Where parting comes no more.

2 Beyond the realm of grief and gloom,
 We then shall rest at home,
Where flowers will forever bloom,
 And storm clouds never come. *Cho.*

3 True worth of soul will there be known,
 Then let us now prepare
To reap what we on earth have sown
 In that bright world so fair. *Cho.*
 B. M. L.

When We Meet Among the Angels.
No. 27. Tune—G. H., No. 74, Vol. III.

"The spirits of just m n."—*Heb.* xii. 23.

1 When we meet among the angels,
 Safe upon the other shore,
In that fair land of to-morrow,
 Free from worldly care and sorrow,
 ||Parting there will come no more ||

CHORUS.
We shall meet, yes, we shall meet,
 Meet upon the peaceful shore;
When we cross the mystic river,
 We shall meet to part no more.

2 When we meet among the angels,
 We shall find our loved ones there.
Joyful then will be the meeting;
Blest indeed will be the greeting
 ||In that world so bright and fair,|| *Cho.*

3 When we meet among the angels,
 We shall chant sweet lays of love,
Where all sing the song of gladness,
Shedding no more tears of sadness,
 ||In that blessed home above,|| *Cho.*

4 When we meet among the angels,
 With a conscience clear and fair,
Having well done all life's labor,
Loved ourselves no more than neighbor,
 ||We shall find a welcome there,|| *Cho.*
 B. M. L.

The True Plan of Salvation.
No. 28. Tune—G. H., No. 28.

"Work out your own."—*Phil.* ii.2.

1 Work out your own salvation
 With fear and trembling too;
Truth will shine clearer, heaven will
  seem nearer,
For each kind deed you do. [skies.
Good never dies; It lives beyond the

CHORUS.
Work out your own salvation,
 No matter what your station;
Work out your own salvation,
 By living just and true.

2 Work out your own salvation;
 No greater joy is known
Than doing duty. Angels of beauty,
 Who worship 'round the throne,
Rejoice to see a soul all pure and free.

3 Work out your own salvation;
 Your life will light the way,
A shining taper unto your neighbor,
 Lest he should go astray; [you take.
Then, for his sake, take care what road

4 Work out your own salvation
 By helping those in need;
Love one another as friend and brother,
 Without respect to creed.
The reign of love is what makes heaven
  above. B. M. L.

The Right Shall Prevail.
No. 29. Tune—G. H., No. 80, Vol. II.

"*On earth, peace.*"—*Luke* ii. 14.

1 When the right over wrong shall prevail,
  When the woe of wine drinking sha'l
    cease;
  Then all nations and people will hail,
  With a shout, the glad tidings of peace.

CHORUS.
It will come by and by,
  When the reign of the rum fiend is o'er.
It will come by and by;
  Then the people will make rum no more.

2 Right ordains that the old wrong must die,
  And make way for the growth of reform;
  Truth and wisdom proclaim from on high
  That the triumph of Temp'rance must
    come. *Cho.*

3 To the bountiful Father of Love
  We will pray that the time soon may
    come
  When the light, as revealed from above,
  Stops the making and drinking of rum.

4 Peace on earth evermore then shall reign,
  And the angels will sing once again,
  While the nations all join the refrain:
    "Peace on earth and good will to all
      men!" B. M. L.

We'll Drink no More.
No. 30. Tune—G. H., No. 22.

"*Keep thyself pure*"—*Tim.* v. 2.

1 Drink wine no more, men by the score
  To graves go down in sorrow;
  Be free to-day, young man it may
  Be too late e'er to-morrow.

CHORUS.
Drink wine no more, drink wine no more,
  Drink wine no more, no, never,
Drink wine no more, drink wine no more,
  Drink wine no more forever. *Cho.*

2 Drink wine no more, life soon is o'er,
  Death may come in youth's morning;
  We sojourn here for one brief year,
  Oh! heed the drunkard's warning. *Cho.*

3 Drink wine no more, beyond the shore
  Free from all sin and sorrow;
  None there will say, in that great day,
  We waited for the morrow. *Cho.*

4 We'll drink no more, the spell is o'er,
  By grace divine we'll sever
  The demon's chain, henceforth the brain
  From wine is free forever.

CHORUS.
We'll drink no more, we'll drink no more,
  We'll drink no more, no, never;
We'll drink no more, we'll drink no more,
  We'll drink no more forever. B. M. L.

Angels Bring Us Peace.
No. 31. Tune—G. H., No. 23.

"*Some have entertained angels.*"—*Heb.* xiii. 1.

1 Come and rejoice that our Father in heav'n
  Unto His angels a mission hath given,
  Bidding them bear these glad tidings
    again, [men.
  Peace and good-will to the children of

CHORUS.
Come and rejoice that the angels above,
  Angels above, angels of love,
Come and rejoice that the angels above
  Bring us sweet peace and love.

2 Loved ones, though gone now, we know
    are not dead,
  When their cold forms in the grave we
    have laid, [same,
  For they still live, and they love us the
  Coming again this grand truth to pro-
    claim. *Cho.*

3 What bliss to know that the beautiful gate
  Stands open wide for the small and the
    great; [low,
  All who have friends still in earth life be-
  Gladly return and their blessings be-
    stow. *Cho.*

4 When we are done with the trials of
    earth,
  We shall receive a reward for our worth;
  Then may we meet, on that ever green
    shore,
  Those that we love, there to part never-
    more. *Cho.* B. M. L.

The Parting Prayer.
No. 32. Tune—G. H., No. 96, Vol. III.

"*Pray with the spirit.*"—*I Cor.* xiv. 15.

1 Supreme Ruler, we implore thee,
  Ere we part a blessing send;
  Henceforth let thy angels lead us,
  Till our lives on earth shall end.

CHORUS.
May the truth that has been spoken
  Find a place in every heart,
And to each soul give some token
  Of thy love before we part.

2 All-wise Author, grant that wisdom
  May direct our thoughts each day,
  And protect us from all evil
  As we journey on life's way. *Cho.*

3 Grant that we again may gather,
  Here as one unbroken band,
  And that each may prove more worthy
  Of sweet friends in Summer Land. *Cho.*

4 Loving Father, let thy angels
  Now unite our hearts as one,
  And as with pure souls in heaven,
  May thy will on earth be done. *Cho.*
  B. M. L.

INDEX.

Title	PAGE
A Beautiful World above	37
Abou Ben Adhem (Chant)	109
A Gentle, Kind Word	34
Alcohol; or, the Pirate Prince	52
All Hail the Time	58
A Name in the Sand	64
A Nation Born Again	57
Angels Bring Us Peace	126
Angel Guide, I Need Thee	79
Angels, Sing Once Again	10
Angels There Will Welcome Thee	7
Angels Whisper They Can Come	121
Aspiration of Purity and Love	49
At Rest in Heaven	19
Back Bone; or, Truth Plainly Told	66
Beyond Life's Troubled Sea	96
Beyond the Beautiful River	121
Break Every Yoke (Chant)	65
Come, Dear Angel Guides	40
Come, Hear the Welcome Voice	81
Crossin' O'er de Ribbah	73
Cross Wins a Crown, The	51
Dare to be Free	74
Death to Alcohol	120
Dora Bell's Pictures	28
Doxologies (Tune, Old Hundred)	87
Dream Faces Celestial	38
Drink No More, My Brother	50
Drink Wine No More	67
Dying Mother's Request, The	56
Evergreen Hills, On the	104
Evergreen Mountains, The	46
Fond Memories of Childhood	89
From the Other Shore	20
Gates Ajar For All, The	120
Gentle, Kind Word, A	34
Glory Thine, The	59
God Bless You	82
Going Home To-morrow	122
Golden Age Draws Nigh, The	122
Golden Day is Dawning, The	84
Golden Gates Are Open, The	72
Golden Years to Come, The	68
Grand Era of Peace, The	70
Great Life Giver, Thou	61
Green Isle of the Ocean	91
Hear the Voice of Truth	123
Heaven is Our Home	123
Hymn of Peace and Progress	12
Inside the Golden Gate	4
In the Sweet Bye and Bye	99
Joyfully Safe at Home	15
Lay Up Treasure in Heaven	124
Lead Me, Loving Angels	83
Lead Us in the Light	120
Learn to do Well	54
Life's Golden Moments	41
Light of That Land, The	124
Mandate of Labor	107
My Country, 'Tis of Thee	35
Name in the Sand, A	64
Nation Born Again, A	57
Nearer, My God, to Thee	124
Ocean Grove Declaration	36
Oh, How Glorious	16
Oh, Think of That Home	64
Old Home of My Childhood, The	97
Old Hundred (Doxologies)	87
One More Loved One Gone	18
On the Evergreen Hills	104
Open the Beautiful Gates	14
Open Wide the Gates	103
Our Father in Heaven (Chant)	35
Our Nation's Glory	88
Over on the Other Shore	85
Parting Prayer, The	126
Parting Song, Good Night	118
Peace Beyond the River	75
Peace on Earth Once More	119
Pilgrim Going Home, The	123
Pilgrim's Daily Prayer, The	47

INDEX.

Title	PAGE
Pilgrim's Invocation, The	6
Pilgrim's Plea for Prayer, The	125
Plowshares of Peace, The	90
Prophet, Tell Us of the Light	71
REMEMBER the Brave Boys	106
Right Shall Prevail, The	126
Rum Maker's Remorse, The	114
SAFE at Home From Sorrow Free	121
Sands of Time are Flowing, The	125
School of Progress, The	76
Set Thy House in Order	92
Ship of Life, The	63
Sing of Love and Peace	93
Soul Has Fled, The	27
Soul's Sweet Home, The	119
Summer Sweets Shall Ever Bloom	78
Sweet Angel Home	23
Sweet Home by the River	9
Sweet Home of the Soul	124
Sweet Hour of Prayer	17
Sweet Land of Sunshine, The	5
Sweet Summer Home	3
Sweet Summer Land	48
Sweet Spirits Can Return	33
TELL Me Not I'm Growing Old	77
Tell Us of the Light	71
Temperance Banner, The	57
Temperance Invocation, The	111
Temperance Ninety and Nine, The	42
That Evergreen Shore	86
That Glorious Rest	8
That Land Beyond the River	26
That Loving Hand is Leading Me	110
That Valley of Peace	119
The Cross Wins a Crown	51
The Dying Mother's Request	56
The Evergreen Mountains	46
The Gate's Ajar for All	120
The Glory Thine	59
The Golden Age Draws Nigh	122
The Golden Day is Dawning	84
The Golden Gates are Open	72
The Golden Years to Come	68
The Grand Era of Peace	70
The Heaving Sea	116
The Light of That Land	124
The Mandate of Labor	107
The Noblest Men	108
The Old Home of My Childhood	97

Title	PAGE
The Parting Prayer	126
The Pilgrim Going Home	123
The Pilgrim's Daily Prayer	47
The Pilgrim's Invocation	6
The Pilgrim's Plea for Prayer	125
The Plowshares of Peace	90
There is Room Among the Angels	80
There to Part No More	122
There We Shall Meet	62
The Right Shall Prevail	126
The Rum Maker's Remorse	114
The Sands of Time are Flowing	125
The School of Progress	76
The Ship of Life	63
The Soul Has Fled	27
The Soul's Sweet Home	119
The Sweet Land of Sunshine	5
The Temperance Banner	57
The Temperance Invocation	111
The Temperance Ninety and Nine	42
The True Plan of Salvation	125
The Voice of Truth	123
The World Hath Felt a Quickening	22
The World Will Be the Better for It	112
The World Would Be the Better for It	113
They Come to Thee	95
Thou Great Life Giver	61
Touch Not, Taste Not, Handle Not	121
VOICE of Truth, The	123
WAITING By the River	27
Waiting for the Morning	32
Waiting in Heaven for Me	100
Walking Through the Valley	98
We Know it Must be True	122
We'll Drink No More	126
We Shall Gather at the River	31
We Shall Know Each Other There	102
We Shall Meet Bye and Bye	120
We Shall Meet Over There	13
We Shall Meet Them Again	24
When We Arrive at Home	11
When We Meet Among the Angels	125
Where Flowers Ever Bloom	119
While On Our Journey Home	43
Who Hath Woe (Chant)	117
Wisdom Better than Gold	44
Wisdom Orders All Things Well	30
Words of Good Cheer	60
World Hath Felt a Quickening, The	22
World Will be the Better for It, The	112
World Would be the Better for It, The	113

J. M. ARMSTRONG & CO.,
MUSIC TYPOGRAPHERS,
710 Sansom Street, Philadelphia, Pa.

www.ingramcontent.com/pod-product-compliance
Lightning Source LLC
Chambersburg PA
CBHW030402170426
43202CB00010B/1459